D0432130

2003

Poems *for* Patriarchs

POEMS *for* PATRIARCHS

THE VERSE AND PROSE OF CHRISTIAN MANHOOD

COMPILED AND EDITED BY
DOUGLAS W. PHILLIPS

"The patriarch hoary,
the sage of his kith
and the hamlet."
—Longfellow

THE VISION FORUM, INC.
SAN ANTONIO, TEXAS

Copyright © 2001 The Vision Forum, Inc.

The Vision Forum, Inc.
4719 Blanco Rd.
San Antonio, Texas 78212
1-800-440-0022
www.visionforum.com

All Rights Reserved.
Written permission must be secured from
the publisher to use or reproduce any part
of this work, except for brief quotations
in critical reviews or articles.

"Where there is no vision, the people perish."

ISBN 1-929241-45-3

Design and Typography by Jeremy M. Fisher

Detail of "Portrait of Baldassare Castiglione,"
before 1516, by Raphael (Raffaello Sanzio, 1483-1520, b. Italy).
Oil on panel, 32 x 26 in., Musée du Louvre, Paris, France.

Printed on acid-free paper
in the United States of America

To Liberty, Jubilee,
and Faith Evangeline

God has given each of you names that carry the hope of the covenant promises of God. From the day you were born, your mother and I lifted each of you to Heaven and begged God to bless you, to make you mighty warriors for Jesus Christ and virtuous women. We have sought, and ever will seek, to raise you with the understanding that the patriarchal vision is not only for men, but also for the great women of God of the 21st century—women who will stand beside their husbands as helpmeets, and communicate to their children a multi-generational vision of faithfulness.

It is my sincere prayer that you will continue to blossom into such women of God, that He will send you men of character and patriarchal vision to be your husbands, and that your own children will someday rise up and call you blessed.

I love you to the moon and back.

Your Devoted Father

OTHER BOOKS FROM VISION FORUM

Missionary Patriarch

Mother

Safely Home

Thoughts for Young Men

The Bible Lessons of John Quincy Adams for His Son

The Letters and Lessons of Teddy Roosevelt for His Sons

The Sinking of the Titanic

Of Plymouth Plantation

The Elsie Dinsmore Series

Cabin on the Prairie

Cabin in the Northwoods

Pollard's Child's History of America

Sergeant York and the Great War

The Life and Campaigns of Stonewall Jackson

*The Boy's Guide to the
Historical Adventures of G.A. Henty*

CONTENTS

INTRODUCTION

The worlds of nature and of providence are full of parallels to things moral and spiritual, and serve as pictures to make the written book of inspiration more clear to the children of God. The Bible itself abounds in metaphors, types and symbols; it is a great picture-book; there is scarcely a poetical figure which may not be found in the law and the prophets, or in the words of Jesus and His apostles. The preacher is bidden to speak the oracles of God, and consequently he should imitate their illustrative method, and abound in emblems and parables. A sermon which is full of 'likes' is full of windows to enlighten the mind and hands to hold it captive. Discourses decked with similes will not only give pleasure to the children, but persons of riper years will be charmed and instructed thereby.

Charles H. Spurgeon

My first exposure to manly poetry came to me as a boy sitting at my father's table. Our dinnertime was noteworthy for the wonderful conversations about current events, the regular readings from biographies and histories, and the obligatory Scripture devotional from the Old and New Testament. On special occasions, my father—a man of distinct patriarchal aspects—would treat us to a rousing poem enunciated in grand manner. We would thrill and sometimes even squeal with delight as Dad would belt out words of heroism, history, sentiment, and bravado from Kipling, Longfellow, and other great poets of the Western world.

Dad carried books of poetry with him while traveling with our family across the country. At appropriate moments, he would draw one of the books from his pocket and wax eloquent in verse. During a family adventure to Alaska, Dad carried a copy of the works of Ronald Reagan's favorite poet, Robert Service. From Ketchican to Sitka to Skagway, Dad baptized our entrance into each new city with Service's chilly poetry of whimsy and adventure from the gold-rush days of the Yukon.

My second introduction to the joy of poetry came when I was a young man in my early twenties. In those days, my father and I frequented a meeting of distinguished statesmen, clergymen, and businessmen who met regularly at diverse locations to discuss current events and public policy. One of the regular attendees, Dr. David Breese, a six-foot seven-inch colossus with a rich baritone voice and enormous hands, took special interest in regaling me for hours with classic poetry of manhood and bravery. (To this day, I have never heard anyone perform "Casey at the Bat" with such vigor and presence.)

Sometimes our recitation sprees lasted past midnight. It came to be a bit of a contest to see if I could stump him by naming a classic poem which he had not committed to memory. I rarely did. But I always went home from those meetings motivated to memorize verse myself, and have, ever since then, incorporated such poems into speeches and sermons.

Requests for these poems have poured into my office for years, so in *Poems for Patriarchs*, I have attempted to compile some of the more inspirational and vision-communicating selections. The collection includes poems and prose both obscure and popular, but selected because of the profound way they speak to the most important issues in a man's life. They are neither fluffy nor frilly, foppish nor foolish, but virile, and often sage, both as to their composition and character. Each chapter in the book contains a generous number of selections, some new, some ancient, but all designed to address the various biblical roles, relationships, and seasons in a man's life, from early boyhood to his twilight years.

Over the years I have come to believe that one reason men lack vision is because they lack poetry in their lives. Men no longer sing or recite inspirational verse. Our boys are no longer required to memorize the great psalms, hymns, and poems of Christian manhood. This should come as no surprise. The 20th century has wreaked havoc upon chivalry and manhood. The transformation of poetry from the ennobling to the coarse, the banal, or the irrelevent is as much a sign of our national loss of manhood as it is of the decline of decency and civilization.

But poetry is essential to a man's life. We should never forget that God chose to communicate through the language of poetry. A large portion of the Scripture from Psalms to The Song of Solomon—even the book of Isaiah in the original language—was written in verse. Why? Because poetry and song allow us to use the beauty of language to paint mental images of victory, of devotion, and of the beauty of life in Jesus Christ.

Poems for Patriarchs was born out of a conviction that the urgent need of the hour is for sturdy men who will sacrificially lead their families with vision. The very concept of patriarchy presupposes faithfulness, service, sacrifice, fatherhood, and multi-generational vision. The collection begins with "Poems of Patriarchy," a section designed to inspire men to think in terms of sacrifice, certitude, and vision. In "Poems of Boyhood," the memories of childhood and glories of being a boy are joyfully proclaimed. "Poems of Sonship" is dedicated to the meaning of honor between father and son. "Poems of the Groom" focuses on a man's love for his bride, and the Lord's love for His bride, the Church. "Poems of Fatherhood" includes some of my favorite poems which remind me of the "big picture" and the glory of raising sons and daughters for the Lord. Many fathers will especially love "Poems for the Children's Hour" and "Poems of Heroism" because they contain some of the very best "daddy read-aloud" poems.

I hope the reader will find among the diverse prose and poetry to follow, ample sources of inspiration and delight to bless the soul and build the family. It is my prayer that this small and unpretentious selection of prose and poetry will serve as a reminder of the greatness of the biblical call for men to be loving fathers, devoted husbands, and true patriarchs of their households.

Douglas W. Phillips
San Antonio, Texas

POEMS OF PATRIARCHY

Praise ye the LORD. Blessed is the man that feareth the LORD, That delighteth greatly in his commandments. His seed shall be mighty upon earth: the generation of the upright shall be blessed. Wealth and riches shall be in his house: and his righteousness endureth for ever. Unto the upright there ariseth light in the darkness: He is gracious, and full of compassion, and righteous. A good man sheweth favour, and lendeth: he will guide his affairs with discretion. Surely he shall not be moved for ever: the righteous shall be in everlasting remembrance. He shall not be afraid of evil tidings: his heart is fixed, trusting in the LORD. His heart is established, he shall not be afraid, until he see his desire upon his enemies. He hath dispersed, he hath given to the poor; His righteousness endureth for ever; his horn shall be exalted with honour. The wicked shall see it, and be grieved; he shall gnash with his teeth, and melt away: The desire of the wicked shall perish.

Psalm 112

Children's children are the crown of old men; and the glory of children are their fathers.

Proverbs 17:6

PATRIARCHY

Where there is no vision, the people perish. Similarly, without vision, the family perishes. The father is the God-ordained vision-communicator for the family. Consequently, without men of vision, there will be no strong families. Capture the father and you win the family.

At the heart of a godly father's vision for his family is the doctrine of biblical patriarchy. As Weldon Hardenbrook has observed, the word patriarch is derived from two Greek words. The first is *patria* (derived from *pater*, "father"), which means "family." The second is *arche*, which means "beginning," "first origin," and "to rule."

A patriarch is the family leader, a household historian, a spiritual shepherd, a defender of children and womankind, and a man with a multi-generational vision. Because patriarchy is inherently life-oriented, godly fathers will rejoice in children and teach them by both word and deed that honoring parents is the key to blessing. Of course, there are perversions of patriarchy with which we would have nothing to do, but biblical patriarchy is central to the long-term success of nations because its foundation is Christ-centered, multi-generational faithfulness.

The wonderful news is that God appears to be igniting the hearts of a growing number of Christian fathers with a hunger to learn more about biblical manhood. This quiet revival is taking place in homes where teary-eyed fathers are standing before their wives and children, repenting for their lack of vision and leadership, and recommitting themselves to God's priorities for bold manhood.

The Patriarchal Vision ❧

THE PATRIARCH

Written during a long train ride en route *to a family reunion, the following poem is dedicated to my wife, Beall, and reflects my own prayer that God would help me to be a faithful father.*

More noble than the valiant deeds of shining knights of yore,
More powerful than earthly plights that make the rich man poor,
More kingly than a royal throne or a lion with his pride,
Is he whose babes sleep well at night sure Daddy will provide.

There is a spirit in this land and Jezebel's her name.
She's calling you to leave your home for power, fun, and fame.
She wants your wife, your children too—she'll never compromise,
Until your house is torn in two by listening to her lies.

But though a hundred thousand million men may fall prey to her lures,
And wives *en masse* leave home in search of "more fulfilling" chores,
Though preachers praise, and friends embrace, her pagan plan of death,
Stand strong and quit you like a man with every blessed breath.

Stand strong and rise, O man of God, to meet this noble call,
The battle is not new you see, it's been here since the Fall.

Your wife is your helpmeet, my friend, and not another man's,
So care for her and keep her far from Mistress Jezi's plans.
Protect, provide, and give to her your undivided life,
This is the dear one of your youth, your precious bride, your wife.

4

And rally to those tiny ones who trust you for their care—
A lifetime spent discipling them's a lifetime pure and rare.
For when they put their hand in yours and know a Daddy's love,
You're showing them a picture of the Father from above.

Look not toward worldly goal or gain, or for your liberty,
Look only into their sweet eyes to find your ministry.
Devote your heart and sacrifice and make your manly mark—
There is none so great as he who finds his call as patriarch.

Douglas W. Phillips

A Christian Home

O give us homes built firm upon the Savior,
Where Christ is Head and Counselor and Guide;
Where every child is taught His love and favor
And gives his heart to Christ, the crucified;
How sweet to know that though his footsteps waver
His faithful Lord is walking by His side.

O give us homes with godly fathers, mothers,
Who always place their hope and trust in Him;
Whose tender patience turmoil never bothers,
Whose calm and courage trouble cannot dim;
A home where each finds joy in serving others,
And love still shines, tho days be dark and grim.

O Lord, our God, our homes are Thine forever!
We trust to Thee their problems, toil, and care;
Their bonds of love no enemy can sever
If Thou art always Lord and Master there:
Be Thou the center of our least endeavor.
Be Thou our Guest, our hearts and homes to share.

Barbara B. Hart

Multi-Generational Faithfulness ❧

WILLIAM BRADFORD'S PILGRIM VISION

The story of the Pilgrims is remarkable in the annals of Christian history because it is the real account of fathers and mothers who left the ease of the city in order to protect their children from the influences of an ungodly youth culture, and who risked their lives, their fortunes, and their sacred honor for the hope of building a multi-generational legacy of faithfulness. Theirs is the ultimate success story, and a testimony to the goodness of God and the wisdom of patriarchy. Remarkably, from the fifty-one people who survived that first cold winter in 1620, more than twenty-million descendants walk the earth today, each of whom can thank their ancestors for making the sacrifices necessary to purchase the liberty we presently enjoy.

Having found a good haven and being brought safely in sight of land, they fell upon their knees and blessed the God of Heaven who had brought them over the cast and furious ocean, and delivered them from all the perils and miseries of it, again to set their feet upon the firm and stable earth, their proper element. And no marvel that they were thus joyful when the wise Seneca was so affected with sailing a few miles off the coast of his own Italy, that he affirmed he

6

had rather taken twenty years to make his way by land, than to go by sea to any place in however short a time,—so tedious and dreadful it was to him.

But here I cannot but make a pause, and stand half amazed at this poor people's present condition; and so I think will the reader, too, when he considers it well. Having thus passed the vast ocean, and that sea of troubles before while they were making their preparations, they now had no friends to welcome them, nor inns to entertain and refresh their weather-beaten bodies, nor houses—much less towns—to repair to.

It is recorded in Scripture (Acts 28) as a mercy to the apostle and his shipwrecked crew, that the barbarians showed them no small kindness in refreshing them; but these savage barbarians when they met with them (as will appear) were readier to fill their sides full of arrows than otherwise! As for the season, it was winter, and those who have experienced the winters of the country know them to be sharp and severe, and subject to fierce storms, when it is dangerous to travel to known places,—much more to search an unknown coast.

Besides, what could they see but a desolate wilderness, full of wild beasts and wild men; and what multitude there might be of them they know not! Neither could they, as it were, go up to the top of Pisgah, to view from this wilderness a more goodly country to feed their hopes; for which way soever they turned their eyes (save upward to the Heavens!) they could gain little solace from any outward objects. Summer being done, all things turned upon them a weather-beaten face; and the whole country, full of woods and thickets, presented a wild and savage view.

If they looked behind them, there was the mighty ocean which they had passed, and was now a gulf separating them from all civilized parts of the world. If it be said that they had their ship to turn to, it is true; but what did they hear daily from the captain and crew? That they should quickly look out for a place with their shallop, where they would be not far off; for the season was such that the captain would not approach nearer to the shore till a harbour had been discovered which he could enter safely; and that the food was being consumed apace, but he must and would keep sufficient for the return voyage. It was even muttered by some of the crew that if they did not find a place in time, they would turn them and their goods ashore and leave them.

Let it be remembered, too, what small hope of further assistance from England they had left behind them, to support their courage in this sad condition and the trials they were under; for how the case stood between the settlers and the merchants at their departure has already been described. It is true, indeed, that the affection and love of their brethren at Leyden towards them was cordial and unbroken; but they had little power to help them or themselves.

What, then, could now sustain them but the spirit of God, and His grace? Ought not the children of their fathers rightly to say: Our fathers were Englishmen who came over the great ocean, and were ready to perish in this wilderness; but they cried unto the Lord, and He heard their voice, and looked on their adversity. . . Let them therefore praise the Lord, because He is good, and His mercies endure forever. Yea, let them that have been redeemed of the Lord, show how he hath delivered them from the hand of the oppressor. When they wandered forth into the desert-wilderness, out of the way, and found no city to dwell in, both hungry and thirsty, their soul was overwhelmed in them. Let them confess before the Lord His loving kindness, and His wonderful works before the sons of men!

William Bradford

Preserving the Ancient Landmarks ❧

DESOLATIONS: VIRGINIA CHURCHES

The Bible commands that we "remove not the ancient landmarks."
Among the greatest of our ancient landmarks are the many colonial
church buildings which to this day remain scattered, often in disrepair,
in remote locations along the colonial coastline. Recently, I visited the
most ancient of America's church buildings, located on the spot in
Jamestown, Virginia, where in 1607, a band of intrepid settlers
committed their work to Jesus Christ and helped to launch a nation.
I was reminded of these haunting words of Arthur Coxe.

I.

Hast been where the full-blossomed bay-tree is blowing,
    With odours like Eden's around?
Hast seen where the broad-leaved palmetto is growing,
    And wild vines are fringing the ground?
Hast sat in the shade of catalpas, at noon,
    To eat the cool gourds of their clime;
Or slept where magnolias were screening the moon,
    And the mocking-bird sung his sweet rhyme?

II.

And didst mark, in thy journey, at dew-dropping eve,
    Some ruin peer high o'er thy way,
With rooks wheeling round it, and ivy to weave
    A mantle for turrets so gray?
Did ye ask if some lord of the cavalier kind
    Lived there, when the country was young?
And burned not the blood of a Christian to find
    How there the old prayer-bell had rung?

III.

And did ye not glow, when they told ye—the Lord
    Had dwelt in that thistle-grown pile;
And that bones of old Christians were under its sward,
    That once had knelt down in its aisle?
And had ye no tear-drops your blushes to steep
    When ye thought—o'er your country so broad,
The bard seeks in vain for a mouldering heap
    Save only these churches of God!

IV.

Oh ye that shall pass by those ruins agen,
    Go kneel in their alleys and pray,
And not till their arches have echoed amen
    Rise up, and fare on, in your way.
Pray God that those aisles may be crowded once more,
    Those altars surrounded and spread,
While anthems and prayers are upsent as of yore,
    As they take of the Chalice and Bread.

V.

Ay, pray on thy knees, that each old rural fane
    They have left to the bat and the mole,
May sound with the loud-pealing organ again,
    And the full-swelling voice of the soul.
Peradventure, when next thou shalt journey thereby,
    Even-bells shall ring out on the air,
And the dim-lighted windows reveal to thine eye
    The snowy-robed pastor at prayer.

Arthur Cleveland Coxe

POEMS OF BOYHOOD

Even a child is known by his doings, whether his work be pure, and whether it be right.

PROVERBS 20:11

Train up a child in the way he should go: and when he is old, he will not depart from it.

PROVERBS 22:6

The father of the righteous shall greatly rejoice: and he that begetteth a wise child shall have joy of him.

PROVERBS 23:24

Boyhood

Once upon a time, boyhood was a cherished season in a man's life: full of purity, possibility, and hope. Part of the patriarchal mission for the 21st century is to restore that sacred window in a boy's life and to rebuild a culture of virtuous and courageous boyhood. A boy must be able to be a boy. He must be given the opportunity to dream big dreams for God—free from the dark images of the modern youth and entertainment culture.

The way a boy plays is ultimately how he will live his life. The heroes he embraces will influence his understanding of nobility and duty. The priorities we set before him in youth will define and determine his priorities as a man. Hence, the profound wisdom of Wordsworth's observation that "the child is the father of the man."

Equally remarkable is the fact that for many of us, the memories of our days as a boy will remain the clearest and the most precious memories of our life, superceding in some cases even the reality of the present. Boyhood is a series of "firsts" that never leave the man. It is a time to wonder, to discover, to laugh, to rejoice, and to believe deeply in the eternal truths of God. I don't know that anyone has ever communicated this truism more beautifully than Arthur Cleveland Coxe in his "Hymn of Boyhood," a remarkable work selected to launch this chapter.

The Panorama of a Boy's Life ❧

THE HYMN OF BOYHOOD

*One thing have I desired of the Lord, which I will require, even that I
may dwell in the house of the Lord all the days of my life, to behold
the fair beauty of the Lord, and to visit his temple.*

PSALTER

I.

The first dear thing that ever I loved
Was a mother's gentle eye,
That smiled, as I woke on the dreamy couch
That cradled my infancy.
I never forget the joyous thrill
That smile in my spirit stirred,
Nor how it could charm me against my will,
Till I laughed like a joyous bird.

II.

And the next fair thing that ever I loved
Was a bunch of summer flowers
With odours, and hues, and loveliness,
Fresh as from Eden's bowers.
I never can find such hues again,
Nor smell such a sweet perfume;
And if there be odours as sweet as them,
'Tis I that have lost the bloom.

III.

And the next dear thing that ever I loved
Was a fawn-like little maid,
Half-pleased, half-awed by the frolic boy
That tortured her doll and played:
I never can see the gossamer
Which rude rough zephyrs tease,
But I think how I tossed her flossy locks
With my whirling bonnets breeze.

IV.

And the next good thing that ever I loved
Was a bow-kite in the sky;
And a little boat on the brooklet's surf,
And a dog for my company,
And a jingling hoop, with many a bound
To my measured strike and true;
And a rocket sent up to the firmament,
When Even was out so blue.

V.

And the next fair thing I was fond to love
Was a field of wavy grain,
Where the reapers mowed; or a ship in sail
On the billow, billowy main.
And the next was a fiery prancing horse
That I felt like a man to stride;
And the next was a beautiful sailing boat
With a helm it was hard to guide.

VI.

And the next dear thing I was fond to love
Is tenderer far to tell;
'Twas a voice, and a hand, and a gentle eye
That dazzled me with its spell:
And the loveliest things I had loved before
Were only the landscape now,
On the canvas bright where I pictured her,
In the glow of my early vow.

VII.

And the next good thing I was fain to love
Was to sit in my cell alone
Musing o'er all these lovely things,
Forever, forever flown.
Then out I walked in the forest free,
Where wantoned the autumn wind
And the coloured boughs swung shiveringly,
In harmony with my mind.

VIII.

And a spirit was on me that next I loved,
That ruleth my spirit still,
And maketh me murmur these sing-song words,
Albeit against my will.
And I walked the woods till the winter came,
And then did I love the snow;
And I heard the gales through the wild wood aisles
Like the Lord's own organ blow.

IX.

And the bush I had loved in my greenwood walk,
I saw it afar away,
Surpliced with snows, like the bending priest
That kneels in the church to pray:
And I thought of the vaulted fane and high,
Where I stood when a little child,
Awed by the lauds sung thrillingly,
And the anthems undefiled.

X.

And again to the vaulted church I went,
And I heard the same sweet prayers,
And the same full organ peals upsent,
And the same soft soothing airs:
And I felt in my spirit so drear and strange,
To think of the race I ran,
That I loved the lone thing that knew no change
In the soul of the boy and man.

XI.

And the tears I wept in the wilderness
And that froze on my lids did fall,
And melted to pearls for my sinfulness
Like scales from the eyes of Paul:
And the last dear thing I was fond to love,
Was that holy service high
That lifted my soul to joys above,
And pleasures that do not die.

XII.

And then, said I, one thing there is
That I of the Lord desire,
That ever while I on earth shall live,
I will of the Lord Require,
That I may dwell in His temple blessed
As long as my life shall be,
And the beauty fair of the Lord of Hosts
In the home of His glory see.

Arthur Cleveland Coxe

❧

THE CHILD IS FATHER OF THE MAN

My heart leaps up when I behold
A rainbow in the sky:
So was it when my life began;
So is it now I am a man;
So be it when I shall grow old,
Or let me die!
The child is father of the man;
And I could wish my days to be
Bound each to each by natural piety.

William Wordsworth

The Memories of Boyhood ❧

THE OLD OAKEN BUCKET

How dear to my heart are the scenes of my childhood,
When fond recollection presents them to view!
The orchard, the meadow, the deep tangled wildwood,
And every loved spot which my infancy knew,
The wide-spreading pond and the mill that stood by it,
The bridge and the rock where the cataract fell;
The cot of my father, the dairy house nigh it,
And e'en the rude bucket that hung in the well.

That moss-covered bucket I hailed as a treasure,
For often at noon, when returned from the field,
I found it the source of an exquisite pleasure,
The purest and sweetest that nature can yield.
How ardent I seized it, with hands that were glowing,
And quick to the white-pebbled bottom it fell.
Then soon, with the emblem of truth overflowing,
And dripping with coolness, it rose from the well.

How sweet from the green, mossy brim to receive it,
As, poised on the curb, it inclined to my lips!
Not a full, blushing goblet could tempt me to leave it,
Tho' filled with the nectar that Jupiter sips.
And now, far removed from the loved habitation,
The tear of regret will intrusively swell,
As fancy reverts to my father's plantation,
And sighs for the bucket that hung in the well.

Samuel Woodworth

19

WOODMAN, SPARE THAT TREE

Woodman, spare that tree!
Touch not a single bough!
In youth it sheltered me,
And I'll protect it now.
'Twas my forefather's hand
That placed it near his cot;
There, Woodman, let it stand,
Thy axe shall harm it not!

That old familiar tree,
Whose glory and renown
Are spread o'er land and sea,
And wouldst thou hew it down?
Woodman, forbear thy stroke!
Cut not its earth-bound ties;
O, spare that aged oak,
Now towering to the skies!

When but an idle boy
I sought its grateful shade;
In all their gushing joy
Here too my sisters played.
My mother kissed me here;
My father pressed my hand—
Forgive this foolish tear,
But let that old oak stand!

My heart-strings round thee cling,
Close as thy bark, old friend!
Here shall the wild-bird sing,
And still thy branches bend.
Old tree! The storm still brave!
And woodman, leave the spot;
While I've a hand to save,
Thy axe shall hurt it not.

George Perkins Morris

The Purity of Boyhood ✣

THE TWO PRAYERS

Last night my little boy
Confessed to me
Some childish wrong;
And kneeling at my knee

He prayed with tears:
"Dear God, make me a man
Like Daddy—wise and strong;
I know You can."

Then while he slept
I knelt beside his bed,
Confessed my sins,
And prayed with low-bowed head,

"O God, make me a child,
Like my child here—
Pure, guileless,
Trusting Thee with faith sincere."

Anonymous

৯

I Have a Boy of Five Years Old

I have a boy of five years old;
His face is fair and fresh to see;
His limbs are cast in beauty's mould,
And dearly he loves me.

One morn we strolled on our dry walk,
Our quiet home all full in view,
And held such intermitted talk
As we are wont to do.

My thoughts on former pleasures ran;
I thought of Kilve's delightful shore,
Our pleasant home when spring began,
A long, long year before.

A day it was when I could bear
Some fond regrets to entertain;
With so much happiness to spare,
I could not feel a pain.

The green earth echoed to the feet
Of lambs that bounded through the glade,
From shade to sunshine, and as fleet
From sunshine back to shade.

Birds warbled round me—and each trace
Of inward sadness had its charm;
Kilve, thought I, was a favored place,
And so is Liswyn farm.

My boy beside me tripped, so slim
And graceful in his rustic dress!
And, as we talked, I questioned him,
In every idleness.

"Now tell me, had you rather be,"
I said, and took him by the arm,
"On Kilve's smooth shore, by the green sea,
Or here at Liswyn farm?"

In careless mood he looked at me,
While still I held him by the arm,
And said, "At Kilve I'd rather be
Than here at Liswyn farm."

"Now, little Edward, say why so:
My little Edward, tell me why."—
"I cannot tell, I do not know."—
"Why, this is strange," said I;

"For here are woods, hills smooth and warm:
there surely must some reason be
Why you would change sweet Liswyn farm
For Kilve by the green sea."

At this my boy hung down his head,
He blushed with shame, nor made reply;
And three times to the child I said,
"Why, Edward, tell me why?"

His head he raised—there was in sight
It caught his eye, he saw it plain—
Upon the house-top, glittering bright,
A broad and gilded vane.

Then did the boy his tongue unlock,
And eased his mind with this reply:
"At Kilve there was no weather-cock;
And that's the reason why."

O dearest, dearest boy! My heart
For better lore would seldom yearn,
Could I but teach the hundredth part
Of what from thee I learn.

William Wordsworth

POEMS OF
SONSHIP

For I was my father's son, tender and only beloved in the sight of my mother.

PROVERBS 4:3

I can of myself do nothing. As I hear, I judge and my judgment is righteous because I do not seek my own will but the will of the father who sent me.

JOHN 5:30

I and my father are one.

JOHN 10:30

Children, obey your parents in the Lord: for this is right. Honor thy father and mother; which is the first commandment with promise; that it may be well with thee, and thou mayest live long on the earth.

EPHESIANS 6:1-3

SONSHIP

The only eternally existing relationship in the universe is that of the Father and the Son (and their relation to the Holy Spirit). There has always been a heavenly Father and an eternal Son. Always. Even "before" (if we can use such linear nomenclature) God created time, there was the Father and the Son. God created earthly father and son relationships so that you and I could understand the love He has for the Son, and the relationship He wants to have with His earthly children (Hebrews 12:5-11).

Perhaps this is one reason why the very last verse of the Old Testament and the first verses of the New Testament which herald the coming of John the Baptist both point to the fact that true revival is linked to fathers turning their hearts to their sons, and sons to their fathers. Note, however, the very first prophecy in the Scripture (Genesis 3:15) concerns Satan's attempt to destroy the godly seed. Because Christ-centered family unity and multi-generational continuity are so central to the perpetuation of the Church, we should not be surprised that a primary focus of Satan's work has been to sever father-son relationships, as evidenced by the national epidemic of boys crying out for their fathers. However, with the rise of father-directed home education and the revival of interest in biblical family life, an increasing number of fathers and sons are turning their hearts to one another. The following poems are dedicated to those men.

The Promise

"Honor thy father, Honor thy mother,"
Shouts the prophet from the grave.
It's the first command with promise
That Jesus ever made.

You may never fully realize,
You may never fully know,
The way this honor transforms
You and all who follow so.

Go to Mom and give your heart.
Go to Dad and give your praise.
Rise up and call them blessed
Who gave to you their days.

There's a power in this adage,
Present from the dawn of time.
For the promise God has given
Is yours to claim and mine.

Douglas W. Phillips

☙

Father of Mine

Father of mine, some years ago
You showed me the way I ought to go;
You led my feet past the treach'rous sand
By the gentle clasp of your own strong hand.

Father of mine, let me thank you for
The prayers you prayed and the burden you bore.
Like a guiding star thro' the tempests' strife,
All your precepts have shone on my path of life.

Father of mine, when the time has passed
And the work of my life is complete at last,
When I step ashore on the glory strand
With a grateful heart I will clasp your hand.

Sarah K. Marinee

◈

I'M STEPPING IN YOUR STEPS

Climbing the mountain wild and high,
Bold was the glance of his eagle eye,
Proud was the spirit that knew no fear,
Reckless the tread of the mountaineer.

Up and up through the fields of snow,
Down and down o'er the rocks below,
On and on o'er the pathway steep,
On o'er the chasms wide and deep.

Hark! O'er the mountain bleak and wild
Echoed the voice of a little child;
"Papa, Look out! I am coming, too,
Stepping in your steps, just like you."

"Papa, O Papa! Just see me,
Walking like Papa—don't you see?"
Pale was the cheek of the mountaineer—
Pale with the thrill of an awful fear;

Paused he quick, and with eager face,
Clasped the child in his strong embrace;
Backward glanced, with his eye so dim,
Back o'er the path he had followed him.

Father, pause in the path of life,
Rough with the chasms of sin and strife;
When you walk with a step so free
'Mong the rocks where the dangers be,

List to the voice that is sounding sweet,
List! They are coming—the little feet.
Walk with care; they are coming too,
"Stepping in your steps, just like you."

Mrs. Avery Stuttle

❧

A Son's Most Precious Inheritance

You got it from your father.
It was all he had to give.
So it's yours to use and cherish
For as long as you may live.

If you lose the tools he gave you
They can always be replaced.
But a black mark on your name, Son,
Can never be erased.

So make sure you guard it wisely
After all is said and done.
You'll be glad your name is spotless
When you give it to your son.

Author Unknown

❧

On Receipt of My Mother's Picture

Oh, that those lips had language! Life has pass'd
With me but roughly since I heard thee last.
Those lips are thine—thy own sweet smiles I see,
The same that oft in childhood solaced me;
Voice only fails, else, how distinct they say,
"Grieve not, my child, chase all thy fears away!"
The meek intelligence of those dear eyes
(Blest be the art that can immortalize,
The art that baffles time's tyrannic claim
To quench it) here shines on me still the same.

Faithful remembrancer of one so dear,
Oh, welcome guest, though unexpected, here!
Who bidd'st me honour with an artless song,
Affectionate, a mother lost so long,
I will obey, not willingly alone,
But gladly, as the precept were her own;
And, while that face renews my filial grief,

Fancy shall weave a charm for my relief—
Shall steep me in Elysian reverie,
A momentary dream, that thou art she.

My Mother! when I learn'd that thou wast dead,
Say, wast thou conscious of the tears I shed?
Hover'd thy spirit o'er thy sorrowing son,
Wretch even then, life's journey just begun?
Perhaps thou gav'st me, though unseen, a kiss;
Perhaps a tear, if souls can weep in bliss—
Ah that maternal smile! it answers—Yes.
I heard the bell toll'd on thy burial day,
I saw the hearse that bore thee slow away,
And, turning from my nurs'ry window, drew
A long, long sigh, and wept a last adieu!

But was it such?—It was.—Where thou art gone
Adieus and farewells are a sound unknown.
May I but meet thee on that peaceful shore,
The parting sound shall pass my lips no more!

Thy maidens griev'd themselves at my concern,
Oft gave me promise of a quick return.
What ardently I wish'd, I long believ'd,
And, disappointed still, was still deceiv'd;
By disappointment every day beguil'd,
Dupe of to-morrow even from a child.
Thus many a sad to-morrow came and went,
Till, all my stock of infant sorrow spent,
I learn'd at last submission to my lot;
But, though I less deplor'd thee, ne'er forgot.

Where once we dwelt our name is heard no more,
Children not thine have trod my nurs'ry floor;

And where the gard'ner Robin, day by day,
Drew me to school along the public way,
Delighted with my bauble coach, and wrapt
In scarlet mantle warm, and velvet capt,
'Tis now become a history little known,
That once we call'd the past'ral house our own.
Short-liv'd possession! but the record fair
That mem'ry keeps of all thy kindness there,
Still outlives many a storm that has effac'd
A thousand other themes less deeply trac'd.
Thy nightly visits to my chamber made,
That thou might'st know me safe and warmly laid;
Thy morning bounties ere I left my home,
The biscuit, or confectionary plum;
The fragrant waters on my cheeks bestow'd
By thy own hand, till fresh they shone and glow'd;
All this, and more endearing still than all,
Thy constant flow of love, that knew no fall,
Ne'er roughen'd by those cataracts and brakes
That humour interpos'd too often makes;
All this still legible in mem'ry's page,
And still to be so, to my latest age,
Adds joy to duty, makes me glad to pay
Such honours to thee as my numbers may;
Perhaps a frail memorial, but sincere,
Not scorn'd in heav'n, though little notic'd here.

Could time, his flight revers'd, restore the hours,
When, playing with thy vesture's tissued flow'rs,
The violet, the pink, and jessamine,
I prick'd them into paper with a pin,
(And thou wast happier than myself the while,
Would'st softly speak, and stroke my head and smile)
Could those few pleasant hours again appear,

Might one wish bring them, would I wish them here?
I would not trust my heart—the dear delight
Seems so to be desir'd, perhaps I might.—
But no—what here we call our life is such,
So little to be lov'd, and thou so much,
That I should ill requite thee to constrain
Thy unbound spirit into bonds again.

Thou, as a gallant bark from Albion's coast
(The storms all weather'd and the ocean cross'd)
Shoots into port at some well-haven'd isle,
Where spices breathe and brighter seasons smile,
There sits quiescent on the floods that show
Her beauteous form reflected clear below,
While airs impregnated with incense play
Around her, fanning light her streamers gay;
So thou, with sails how swift! hast reach'd the shore
"Where tempests never beat nor billows roar,"
And thy lov'd consort on the dang'rous tide
Of life, long since, has anchor'd at thy side.
But me, scarce hoping to attain that rest,
Always from port withheld, always distress'd—
Me howling winds drive devious, tempest toss'd,
Sails ript, seams op'ning wide, and compass lost,
And day by day some current's thwarting force
Sets me more distant from a prosp'rous course.
But oh the thought, that thou art safe, and he!
That thought is joy, arrive what may to me.
My boast is not that I deduce my birth
From loins enthron'd, and rulers of the earth;
But higher far my proud pretensions rise—
The son of parents pass'd into the skies.
And now, farewell—time, unrevok'd, has run
His wonted course, yet what I wish'd is done.

By contemplation's help, not sought in vain,
I seem t' have liv'd my childhood o'er again;
To have renew'd the joys that once were mine,
Without the sin of violating thine:
And, while the wings of fancy still are free,
And I can view this mimic shew of thee,
Time has but half succeeded in his theft—
Thyself remov'd, thy power to sooth me left.

William Cowper

❧

POEMS OF FATHERHOOD

"…to turn the hearts of the fathers to their children and the disobedient to the wisdom of the righteous— to make ready a people prepared for the Lord."
MALACHI 4:6; LUKE 1:17

"Then answered Jesus and said unto them, Verily, verily, I say unto you, The Son can do nothing of himself, but what he seeth the father do: for what things soever he doeth, these also doeth the Son likewise. For the Father loveth the Son, and sheweth him all things that himself doeth…"
JOHN 5:18

FATHERHOOD

Patriarchy presupposes a passion for children. The promise from God to Abraham that He would multiply this man's progeny and make them mighty on the earth was a defining motivation in Abraham's life. Historically, men of God have longed to be fathers and they have craved children—lots of them. The more, the better. Children were perceived as a source of blessing, a source of wealth, and a tool for advancing the Kingdom of God. The Bible even describes them as the godly man's "reward."

But fatherhood is about much more than simply having children. It is about shepherding them and raising them to be covenant keepers. The beauty of Christian fatherhood is that success is not rooted in intellectual prowess, educational background, or social status; but rather in the desire of a man to be faithful to the Word of God.

The following poems examine the oft-neglected but most important aspects of a man's fatherhood: His role as a tender shepherd, leading his children to the Throne of Grace. His mission as the individual primarily responsible for shaping the lives of future men and women. And his life-long quest to lead his children by communicating with passion a vision of service to King Jesus.

The Father as Shepherd ❧

WHEN FATHER PRAYS

When father prays he doesn't use
The words the preacher does;
There's different things for different days—
But mostly it's for us.

When father prays the house is still,
His voice is slow and deep.
We shut our eyes, the clock ticks loud,
So quiet we must keep.

He prays that we may be good boys,
And later on, good men;
And then we squirm, and think we won't
Have any quarrels again.

You'd never think to look at Dad
He once had tempers too.
I guess if father needs to pray,
We youngsters surely do.

Sometimes the prayer gets very long
And hard to understand,
And then I wiggle up quite close,
And let him hold my hand.

I can't remember all of it—
I'm little yet, you see;
But one thing I cannot forget—
My father prays for me.

Unknown

ॐ

When Father Reads the Book

In these days of rush and bustle
When we hurry off to work,
I'm reminded of those early times
When father read the Book.
When father read the Book.
As we each our places took
Round the dear old family altar
When father read the Book.

O those dear old Bible stories,
Psalms that flowed like rippling brook;
Warnings, promises, and precepts
Lived, as father read that Book.
As father read the Book.
Satan's kingdom round us shook,
And our Savior early claimed us
Because father read the Book.

O they say it was old-fashioned,
And what waste of time 'twould look
To now take half-an-hour
To let father read the Book.
But as father read the Book,
Blessed thought in our minds stuck;
And the day went so much better
Just 'cause father read the Book.

Oft I'm troubled as I journey
On toward heav'n with upward look,
To see families all about me
Grow up without father's Book.
Let father read the Book,
Kneel and pray and read the Book;
Your home will be so different
If your father reads the Book.

G.E. Foster

❧

MY PRAYER

Father, today I bring to Thee
This boy of mine whom Thou hast made.
In everything he looks to me,
In turn, I look to Thee for aid.

He knows not all that is before;
He little dreams of hidden snares.
He holds my hand, and o'er and o'er
I find myself beset with fears.

Father, as this boy looks to me
For guidance, and my help implores,
I bring him now in prayer to Thee;
He trusts my strength, and I trust Yours.

Hold Thou my hand as I hold his,
And so guide me that I may guide.
Teach me, Lord, that I may teach,
And keep me free from foolish pride.

Help me to help this boy of mine.
To be to him a father true,
Hold me, Lord, for everything
As fast as I hold my boy for You.

Nauzon W. Braphamm

The Father as Shaper of Future Men ❧

WANTED: A MAN TO LEAD

There isn't a boy but wants to grow
Manly and true at heart,
And every lad would like to know
The secrets we can impart.
He doesn't want to slack or shirk—
Oh, haven't you heard him plead?
He'll follow a man at play or work
If only the man will lead.

Where are the men to lead today,
Sparing an hour or two,
Teaching the boy the game to play
Just as a man should do?
Village and slums are calling—"Come,
Here are the boys!" Indeed,
Who can tell what they might become
If only the man would lead.

Where are the men to lend a hand?
Echo it far and wide—
Men who will rise in every land,
Bridging the "Great Divide."
Nation and flag and tongue unite
Joining each class and creed.
Here are the boys who would do right—
But where are the men to lead?

Wesleyan Methodist

❧

To Any Boy's Father

There are little eyes upon you,
And they're watching night and day;
There are little ears that quickly
Take in every word you say.
There are little hands all eager
To do everything you do,
And a little boy who's dreaming
Of the day he'll be like you.

You're the little fellow's hero,
You're the wisest of the wise:
In his little mind, about you,
No suspicions ever rise.
He believes in you devoutly,
Holds that all you say and do,
He will say and do in your way
When he's grown up just like you.

There's a wide-eyed little fellow,
Who believes you're always right;
And his ears are always open
And he watches day and night.
You are setting an example
Every day in all you do,
For the little boy who's waiting
To grow up to be like you!

Unknown

๕

THE CHAP AT HOME

To feel his little hand in mine,
So clinging and so warm,
To know he thinks me strong enough
To keep him safe from harm:
To see his simple faith in all
That I can say or do;
It sort o' shames a fellow,
But it makes him better, too.
And I'm trying hard to be the man
He fancies me to be,
Because I have this chap at home
Who thinks the world of me.

I would not disappoint his trust
For anything on earth,
Nor let him know how little I
Just naturally am worth.
But after all, it's easier
That brighter road to climb,
With the little hands behind me
To push me all the time.
And I reckon I'm a better man
Than what I used to be
Because I have this chap at home
Who thinks the world of me.

Unknown

The Father as Visionary ❧

To My Unborn Son

"My SON!" What simple, beautiful words!
"My boy!" What a wonderful phrase!
We're counting the months till you come to us—
The months, and the weeks, and the days!

"The new little stranger," some babes are called,
But that's not what you're going to be;
With double my Virtues and half of my faults,
You can't be a stranger to me!

Your mother is straight as a sapling plant,
The cleanest and best of her clan—
You're bone of her bone, and flesh of her flesh,
And, by heaven, we'll make you a man!

Soon I shall take you in two strong arms—
You that shall howl for joy—
With a simple, passionate, wonderful pride
Because you are just—my boy!

And you shall lie in your mother's arms,
And croon at your mother's breast,
And I shall thank God I am there to shield
The two that I love the best.

A wonderful thing is a breaking wave,
And sweet is the scent of spring,
But the silent voice of an unborn babe
Is God's most beautiful thing.

We're listening now to that silent voice
And waiting, your mother and I—
Waiting to welcome the fruit of our love
When you come to us by and by.

We're hungry to show you a wonderful world
With wonderful things to be done,
We're aching to give you the best of us both
And we're lonely for you—my son!

Captain Cyril Morton Thorne

୬

A FATHER'S PRAYER

Lord, strengthen me that I may be
A fit example for my son.
Grant he may never hear or see
A shameful deed that I have done.
How ever sorely I am tried,
Let me not undermine his pride.

Lord, make me tolerant and wise,
Incline my ears to hear him through.
Let him not stand with downcast eyes
Fearing to trust me and be true.
Instruct me so that I may know
The way my son and I should go.

When he shall err as once I did,
Or boyhood's folly bids him stray,
Let me not into anger fly
And drive the good in him away.
Teach me to win his trust—that he
Shall keep no secret hid from me.

Lord, as his father now I pray
For manhood's strength and counsel wise,
Let me deal justly day by day,
In all that fatherhood implies.
To be his father, keep me fit,
Let me not play the hypocrite.

Edgar Guest

๛

ONLY A DAD

Only a dad with a tired face,
Coming home from the daily race,
Bringing little of gold or fame
To show how well he has played the game;
But glad in his heart that his own rejoice
To see him come and to hear his voice.

Only a dad with a brood of four,
One of ten million men or more
Plodding along in the daily strife,
Bearing the whips and the scorns of life,
With never a whimper of pain or hate,
For the sake of those who at home await.

Only a dad, neither rich nor proud,
Merely one of the surging crowd,
Toiling, striving from day to day,
Facing whatever may come his way,
Silent whenever the harsh condemn,
And bearing it all for the love of them.

Only a dad but he gives his all,
To smooth the way for his children small,
Doing with courage stern and grim
The deeds that his father did for him.
This is the line that for him I pen:
Only a dad, but the best of men.

Edgar Guest

❧

There's a Land of Beginning Again

I wish that there were some wonderful place
Called "The Land of Beginning Again,"
Where all our mistakes and all our heartaches
And all our poor, selfish griefs
Could be dropped, like a shabbly old coat, at the door
And never be put on again.

I wish we could come on it all unaware,
Like the hunter who finds a lost trail;
And I wish that the one whom our blindness had done
The greatest injustice of all,
Could be at the gate like an old friend who waits
For the comrade he's gladdest to hail.

We would find all the things we intended to do
But forgot, and remembered too late—
Little praises unspoken, little promises broken,
And all of the thousand and one
Little duties neglected that might have perfected
The days of the less fortunate.

It wouldn't be possible not to be kind
In "The Land of Beginning Again,"
And the one we misjudge, and the one whom we grudged
Their moments of victory here,
Would find the grasp of our loving handclasp
More than penitent lips could explain.

For what had been hardest, we'd know had been best,
And what had seemed loss would be gain,
And there isn't a sting that wouldn't take wing,
When we'd face it and laugh it away,
And I think that laughter is most what we're after,
In "The Land of Beginning Again."

So, I'm glad I've embraced that wonderful place
Called "The Land of Beginning Again,"
It's where faith turns to sight, and there is no more night,
For the Lord makes the day never end;
Where all our mistakes and all our heartaches
And all our poor, selfish griefs
Could be dropped, like a ragged, old coat at the door,
And never be put on again.

There's a wonderful place for the whole human race
Called "The Land of Beginning Again;"
Where the acts of the past, in forgiveness cast,
Rise no more, for God's pardon we gain!
And the Savior we find, who will always be kind
As the King of our hearts, He shall reign.
And though sin-sick and sad, we will always be glad,
In "The Land of Beginning Again."

The old life we can stop, just the same as we drop
A shabby old coat at the door,
With it all to be through; we can put on the "new,"
And discard the old rags evermore.
Standing there at the gates, the Omnipotent waits,
And His suffering we cannot disdain—
Wounded hands, feet and side, and we all may abide
In "The Land of Beginning Again."

Aims to magnify self are all laid on the shelf,
While the best of love's service we give,
As we seek so we find, every chance to be kind
In the interests of others to live.
And if unmeant mistakes should cause any heartaches,
Their forgiveness we soon would obtain,
For God's Love reigns supreme, in our lives it would gleam
In "The Land of Beginning Again."

How tranquil the earth, with the new second birth;
For all people would live "on the square,"
And each hold the other, as he would be brother,
And in all of his dealings be fair,
Then all strife and unrest would give way to love's quest
And sweet peace and prosperity reign,
For the trumpets of war sound their call nevermore
In "The Land of Beginning Again."

There is no magic way that in sin we may stay,
And that beautiful land hope to win.
To us God's Word is sent, that we all must repent,
And accept His Salvation from sin.
Oh, the sun is so bright and our hearts are so light,
When we move from sin's evil domain,
And we start on the road to take up our abode
In "The Land of Beginning Again."

Irena Arnold & Louisa Fletcher

❧

Poems of the Groom

For as a young man marrieth a virgin, So shall thy sons marry thee: And as the bridegroom rejoiceth over the bride, So shall thy God rejoice over thee.

ISAIAH 62:5

The voice of joy, and the voice of gladness, The voice of the bridegroom, and the voice of the bride, The voice of them that shall say, Praise the LORD of hosts: For the LORD is good; for his mercy endureth for ever.

JEREMIAH 33:11

And I John saw the holy city, New Jerusalem, Coming down from God out of Heaven, Prepared as a bride adorned for her husband.

REVELATION 21:2

THE GROOM

Next in importance to the relationship of the heavenly Father to the heavenly Son is that of the eternal Groom to his beloved Bride. Upon this relationship all earthly marriages are to be modeled.

We are told in Scripture that as Christ loved His bride, so are men to love their wives. For this reason, we will never have a resurgence of biblical patriarchy unless we first understand Christ's love for the Church, His willingness to die for her, and His promise to provide, protect, and lead her in all things. In fact, at the very heart of the patriarchal mission is the unity a man experiences with his bride and the commitment he willingly embraces to daily lay down his life for her.

The following chapter offers selections which portray aspects of a groom's holy love for his bride. The chapter begins with the eternal Groom's courtship of His bride. It includes Spurgeon's rich vision for the blessed marriage. Next, using the poignant words of men facing death and separation from their beloved, it reveals the meaning of deep abiding love and true commitment which a man must have for his helpmeet.

The Blessed Marriage ❧

SONG OF SOLOMON
SELECTIONS FROM CHAPTER SIX

Whither is thy beloved gone,
O thou fairest among women?
Whither is thy beloved turned aside?
That we may seek him with thee.

My beloved is gone down into his garden,
To the beds of spices,
To feed in the gardens,
And to gather lilies.

I am my beloved's, and my beloved is mine:
He feedeth among the lilies.

Thou art beautiful, O my love,
As Tirzah, comely as Jerusalem,
Terrible as an army with banners.

Turn away thine eyes from me,
For they have overcome me:
Thy hair is as a flock of goats that appear from Gilead.

Thy teeth are as a flock of sheep which go up from the washing,
Whereof every one beareth twins,
And there is not one barren among them.

As a piece of a pomegranate are thy temples within thy locks.
There are threescore queens, and fourscore concubines,
And virgins without number.

My dove, my undefiled is but one;
She is the only one of her mother,
She is the choice one of her that bare her.

The daughters saw her, and blessed her;
Yea, the queens and the concubines,
And they praised her.

Who is she that looketh forth as the morning,
Fair as the moon, clear as the sun,
And terrible as an army with banners?

Return, return, O Shulamite;
Return, return, that we may look upon thee.
What will ye see in the Shulamite?
As it were the company of two armies.

❧

THE CHRISTIAN MARRIAGE

Sometimes we have seen a model marriage, founded on pure love, and cemented in mutual esteem. Therein, the husband acts as a tender head; and the wife, as a true spouse, realizes the model marriage-relation, and sets forth what our oneness with the Lord ought to be. She delights in her husband, in his person, his character, his affection; to her, he is not only the chief and foremost of mankind, but in her eyes he is all-in-all; her heart's love belongs to him, and to him only. She finds sweetest content and solace in his company, his fellowship, his fondness; he is her little world, her Paradise, her choice treasure. At any time, she would gladly lay aside her own pleasure to find it doubled in gratifying him. She is glad to sink her individuality in his. She seeks no renown for herself; his honor is reflected upon her, and she rejoices in it. She would defend his name with her dying breath; safe enough is he where she can speak for him. The domestic circle is her kingdom; that she may there create happiness and comfort is her lifework; and his smiling gratitude is all the reward she seeks. Even in her dress, she thinks of him; without constraint she consults his taste and considers nothing beautiful which is distasteful to him.

A tear from his eye, because of any unkindness on her part, would grievously torment her. She asks not how her behavior may please a stranger, or how another's judgment may approve her conduct; let her beloved be content, and she is glad. He has many objects in life, some of which she does not quite understand; but she believes in them all, and anything she can do to promote them, she delights to perform. He lavishes love on her, and, in return, she lavishes love on him. Their object in life is common. There are points where their affections so intimately united that none could tell which is first and which is second. To watch their children growing up in health and strength, to see them holding posts of usefulness and honor, is their mutual concern; in this and other matters, they are fully one. Their wishes blend, their hearts are indivisible. By degrees, they come to think very much the same thoughts. Intimate association creates conformity; I have known this to become so complete that, at the same moment, the same utterance has leaped to both their lips.

Happy woman and happy man! If Heaven be found on earth, they have it! At last, the two are so blended, so engrafted on one stem, that their old age presents a lovely attachment, a common sympathy, by which its infirmities are greatly alleviated, and its burdens are transformed into fresh bonds of love. So happy a union of will, sentiment, thought, and heart exists between them, that the two streams of their life have washed away the dividing bank, and run on as one broad current of united existence till their common joy falls into the ocean of eternal felicity.

Charles H. Spurgeon

Love of the Bride ❧

THE BATTLEFIELD LETTER OF SULLIVAN BALLOU
TO HIS BRIDE SARAH. MAILED ON JULY 14, 1861,
JUST DAYS BEFORE HIS DEATH.

My Very Dear Sarah,

The indications are very strong that we will move in a few days—perhaps tomorrow. Lest I should not be able to write you again, I feel impelled to write a few lines that may fall under your eye when I shall be no more.

Our movement may be one of a few days duration and full of pleasure—or it may be one of severe conflict and death to me. Not my will, but thine, O God, be done. If it is necessary that I should fall on the battlefield for my country, I am ready. I have no misgivings about, or lack of confidence in, the cause in which I am engaged, and my courage does not halt or falter. I know how strongly American Civilization now leans upon the triumph of the government, and how great a debt we owe to those who went before us through the blood and suffering of the Revolution. And I am willing—perfectly willing—to lay down all my joys in this life to help maintain this government, and to pay that debt.

But, my dear wife, when I know that with my own joys I lay down nearly all of yours, and replace them in this life with cares and sorrows—when, after having eaten for long years the bitter fruit of orphanage myself, I must offer it as their only sustenance to my dear little children—is it weak or dishonorable, while the banner of my purpose floats calmly and proudly in the breeze, that my unbounded love for you, my darling wife and children, should struggle in fierce, though useless, contest with my love of country?

I cannot describe to you my feelings on this calm summer night, when two thousand men are sleeping around me, many of them

61

enjoying the last, perhaps, before that of death—and I, suspicious that Death is creeping behind me with his fatal dart, am communing with God, my country, and thee.

I have sought most closely and diligently, and often in my breast, for a wrong motive in thus hazarding the happiness of those I loved, and I could not find one. A pure love of my country and the principles I have often advocated before the people and "the name of honor that I love more than I fear death" have called upon me, and I have obeyed.

Sarah, my love for you is deathless, it seems to bind me to you with mighty cables that nothing but Omnipotence could break; and yet my love of Country comes over me like a strong wind and bears me irresistibly on, with all these chains, to the battlefield.

The memories of the blissful moments I have spent with you come creeping over me, and I feel most gratified to God and to you that I have enjoyed them so long. And hard for me it is to give them up and burn to ashes the hopes of future years when, God willing, we might still have lived and loved together, and seen our sons grow up to honorable manhood around us. I have, I know, but few and small claims upon Divine Providence, but something whispers to me— perhaps it is the wafted prayer of my little Edgar—that I shall return to my loved ones unharmed. If I do not, my dear Sarah, never forget how much I love you, and when my last breath escapes me on the battlefield, it will whisper your name.

Forgive my many faults, and the many pains I have caused you. How thoughtless and foolish I have often times been! How gladly would I wash out with my tears every little spot upon your happiness, and struggle with all the misfortune of this world, to shield you and my children from harm. But I cannot. I must watch you from the spirit land and hover near you, while you buffet the storms with your precious little freight, and wait with sad patience till we meet to part no more.

But, O Sarah! If the dead can come back to this earth and flit unseen around those they loved, I shall always be near you; in the garish day and in the darkest night—amidst your happiest scenes and gloomiest hours—always, always; and if there be a soft breeze upon your cheek, it shall be my breath; or the cool air fans your throbbing temple, it shall be my spirit passing by.

Sarah, do not mourn me dead; think I am gone and wait for thee, for we shall meet again.

As for my little boys, they will grow as I have done, and never know a father's love and care. Little Willie is too young to remember me long, and my blue-eyed Edgar will keep my frolics with him among the dimmest memories of his childhood. Sarah, I have unlimited confidence in your maternal care and your development of their characters. Tell my two mothers his and hers I call God's blessing upon them.

O Sarah, I wait for you there! Come to me, and lead thither my children.

ॐ

SAMUEL RUTHERFORD'S LOVE FOR THE BRIDE
"THE SANDS OF TIME"

Through his landmark work, Lex Rex, *Rutherford brilliantly articulated the biblical doctrine of resistance against unlawful authority. For his heroic stance, he was placed under house arrest and was awaiting possible execution, but died before his captors could retrieve him. The following poem was inspired by his last words.*

> The sands of time are sinking,
>   The dawn of Heaven breaks,
> The summer morn I've sighed for,
>   The fair sweet morn awakes:
> Dark, dark hath been the midnight,
>   But dayspring is at hand,
> And glory—glory dwelleth.
>   In Immanuel's land.

Oh! well it is for ever,
　　Oh! well for evermore,
My nest hung in no forest
　　Of all this death-doom'd shore
Yea, let the vain world vanish,
　　As from the ship the strand,
While glory—glory dwelleth
　　In Immanuel's land.

There the Red Rose of Sharon
　　Unfolds its heartsome bloom,
And fills the air of Heaven
　　With ravishing perfume:—
Oh! to behold it blossom,
　　While by its fragrance fann'd,
Where glory—glory dwelleth
　　In Immanuel's land.

The King there in His beauty,
　　Without a veil, is seen:
It were a well-spent journey,
　　Though seven deaths lay between.
The Lamb, with His fair army,
　　Doth on Mount Zion stand,
And glory—glory dwelleth
　　In Immanuel's land.

Oh! Christ He is the Fountain,
    The deep sweet well of love!
The streams on earth I've tasted,
    More deep I'll drink above:
There, to an ocean fullness,
    His mercy doth expand,
And glory—glory dwelleth
    In Immanuel's land.

E'en Anwoth was not heaven—
    E'en preaching was not Christ
And in my sea-beat prison
    My Lord and I held tryst:
And aye my murkiest storm-cloud
    Was by a rainbow spann'd,
Caught from the glory dwelling
    In Immanuel's land.

But that He built a heaven
    Of His surpassing love,
A little New Jerusalem,
    Like to the one above,—
"Lord, take me o'er the water,"
    Had been my loud demand,
"Take me to love's own country,
    Unto Immanuel's land."

But flowers need night's cool darkness,
    The moonlight and the dew;
So Christ, from one who loved it,
    His shining oft withdrew;
And then for cause of absence,
    My troubled soul I scann'd—
But glory, shadeless, shineth
    In Immanuel's land.

The little birds of Anwoth
    I used to count them blest,—
Now, beside happier altars
    I go to build my nest:
O'er these there broods no silence,
    No graves around them stand,
For glory, deathless, dwelleth
    In Immanuel's land.

Fair Anwoth by the Solway,
    To me thou still art dear!
E'en from the verge of Heaven
    I drop for thee a tear.
Oh! if one soul from Anwoth
    Meet me at God's right hand,
My Heaven will be two Heavens,
    In Immanuel's land.

I have wrestled on towards Heaven,
　　'Gainst storm, and wind, and tide:—
Now, like a weary traveller,
　　That leaneth on his guide,
Amid the shades of evening,
　　While sinks life's ling'ring sand,
I hail the glory dawning
　　From Immanuel's land.

Deep waters cross'd life's pathway,
　　The hedge of thorns was sharp
Now these lie all behind me—
　　Oh! for a well-tuned harp!
Oh! to join Halleluiah
　　With yon triumphant band,
Who sing, where glory dwelleth,
　　In Immanuel's land.

With mercy and with judgment
　　My web of time He wove,
And aye the dews of sorrow
　　Were lustred with His love.
I'll bless the hand that guided,
　　I'll bless the heart that plann'd,
When throned where glory dwelleth
　　In Immanuel's land.

Soon shall the cup of glory
   Wash down earth's bitterest woes,
Soon shall the desert-briar
   Break into Eden's rose:
The curse shall change to blessing—
   The name on earth that's bann'd,
Be graven on the white stone
   In Immanuel's land.

Oh! I am my Beloved's,
   And my Beloved is mine!
He brings a poor vile sinner
   Into His "House of wine."
I stand upon His merit,
   I know no other stand,
Not e'en where glory dwelleth
   In Immanuel's land.

I shall sleep sound in Jesus,
   Fill'd with His likeness rise,
To live and to adore Him,
   To see Him with these eyes.
'Tween me and resurrection
   But Paradise doth stand;
Then—then for glory dwelling
   In Immanuel's land!

The Bride eyes not her garment,
    But her dear Bridegroom's face
I will not gaze at glory,
    But on my King of Grace—
Not at the crown He gifteth,
    But on His piercèd hand:—
The Lamb is all the glory
    Of Immanuel's land.

I have borne scorn and hatred,
    I have borne wrong and shame,
Earth's proud ones have reproach'd me,
    For Christ's thrice blessed name:—
Where God His seal set fairest
    They've stamp'd their foulest brand;
But judgment shines like noonday
    In Immanuel's land.

They've summoned me before them,
    But there I may not come,—
My Lord says, "Come up hither,"
    My Lord says, "Welcome Home!"
My kingly King, at His white throne,
    My presence doth command,
Where glory—glory dwelleth
    In Immanuel's land.

Mrs. A.R. Cousin

≥ò.

THE FAREWELL LETTER OF CHRISTOPHER LOVE
TO HIS BRIDE ON THE OCCASION OF HIS EXECUTION

Before his execution for an alleged role in a plot to restore Charles II to the throne of England, Christopher Love wrote one final letter to his beloved wife. The letter is a remarkable example of genuine Christian self-denial and charity between a husband and wife. True to his name, Love demonstrates that even in death, her welfare is his chief concern. His sage advice on how to serve Christ as a mother and widow is a testimony to husbands of any century.

My Most Gracious Beloved,

I am now going from a prison to a palace: I have finished my work, and am now going to receive my wages. I am going to heaven, where are two of my children, and leaving you on earth, where there are three of my babes. These two above, need not my care; but the three below need thine. It comforts me to think, two of my children are in the bosom of Abraham, and three of them will be in the arms and care of such a tender and godly mother. I know you are a woman of sorrowful spirit, yet be comforted, though your sorrows be great for your husband going out of the world, yet your pains shall be the less in bringing your child into the world; you shall be a joyful mother, though you be a sad widow; God hath many mercies in store for you; the prayer of a dying husband for you will not be lost. To my shame I speak it, I never prayed for you at liberty, as I have done in prison. I can write much, but I have few practical counsels to leave with you, viz.,

1. Keep under a sound, orthodox, soul searching ministry. Oh! There are many deceivers gone out into the world, but Christ's sheep know His voice, and a stranger they will not follow. Attend any minister that teacheth the way of God in truth; and follow Solomon's advice, Proverbs 19:27.

2. Bring up your children in the knowledge and admonition of the Lord. The mother ought to be a teacher in the father's absence,

Proverbs 31:1, "The words that his mother taught him…" And Timothy was instructed by his grandmother, 1 Timothy 1:5.

3. Pray in your family daily, that yours may be in the number of the families who call upon God.

4. Labor for a meek and quiet spirit, which in the sight of God, is of great price, 1 Peter 3:4.

5. Pour not on the comforts you want, but upon the mercies you have. Look rather at God's ending in afflicting, than to the measure and degree of your affliction.

6. Labor to clear up your evidence for heaven when God takes from you the comfort of earth, so that as your sufferings do abound, your consolation in Christ may abound much more, 2 Corinthians 1:5. Though it be good to maintain a holy jealousy of heart, yet it is still ill of you to cherish fears and doubts touching the truth of your graces. If ever I had confidence touching the grace of another, I have confidence of grace in you; as Peter said of Silvanus, I am persuaded that this is the grace of God wherein ye stand, 1 Peter 5:12.

7. O, my dear soul wherefore dost thou doubt, whose heart has been laid upright, whose walking has been holy, &c. I could venture my soul this day in thy soul's stead, such a confidence I have in you.

8. When you find your heart secure, presumptuous and proud, then pour upon corruption more than grace: then look upon your grace without infirmities.

9. Study the covenant of grace, and merits of Christ, and be troubled if you can; you are interested in such a covenant that accepts purposes for performances, desires for deeds, sincerity for perfection, the righteousness of another, viz., that of Jesus Christ, as it were your own alone. Oh! My love! Rest thou in the love of God, the bosom of Christ.

10. Swallow up your will in the will of God. It is a bitter cup we are to drink, but it is the cup of our Father which has been put into our hands. When Paul was to suffer at Jerusalem, the Christians said, "The will of the Lord be done!" Oh! Say ye so, when I go to the Tower-Hill, "The will of the Lord be done!"

11. Rejoice in my joy. To mourn for me inordinately argues, that

you either envy or suspect my happiness. The joy of the Lord is my strength; Oh! Let it be yours also! Dear wife, farewell: I will call thee wife no more: I shall see thy face no more: yet I am not much troubled, for now I am going to meet the Bridegroom, the Lord Jesus, to whom I shall be eternally married.

12. Refuse not to marry, when God offers you a fair opportunity; but be sure you marry in the Lord; and one of a good disposition, that he may not grieve you, but give you a comfortable livelihood in the world.

Farewell dear love, and again I say farewell. The Lord Jesus be with your spirit, the Maker of heaven and earth be a husband to you; and the Father of the Lord Jesus Christ be a father to your children—so prays your dying,

Your most affectionate friend till death,
Christopher Love
The day of my glorification.
From the Tower of London, August 22, 1651

Poems of
Heroism and
Bravery

And what shall I more say? For the time would fail me to tell of Gideon, and of Barak, and of Samson, and of Jephthae; of David also, and Samuel, and of the prophets: Who through faith subdued kingdoms, wrought righteousness, obtained promises, stopped the mouths of lions. Quenched the violence of fire, escaped the edge of the sword, out of weakness were made strong, waxed valiant in fight, turned to flight the armies of the aliens . . . And others had trial of cruel mockings and scourgings, yea, moreover of bonds and imprisonment: They were stoned, they were sawn asunder, were tempted, were slain with the sword: they wandered about in sheepskins and goatskins; being destitute, afflicted, tormented; (Of whom the world was not worthy) they wandered in deserts, and in mountains, and in dens and caves of the earth. And these all, having obtained a good report through faith, received not the promise: God having provided some better thing for us, that they without us should not be made perfect.

HEBREWS 11

Heroism and Bravery

In the first book to the Corinthians, the Apostle Paul writes: "Watch ye, stand fast in the faith. Quit you like men. Be strong." In fact, the Holy Scriptures are replete with admonitions for men to stand fast and to act with a bravery and courage which emanates from a deep abiding confidence in the Lord. In Scripture, we learn that the godly man will stand fast in all circumstances because his confidence is in the Lord of hosts.

For thousands of years, God has raised up heroes to defend truth, to build walls, to act sacrificially on behalf of women and children, and even to bear arms in defense of the innocent. The common denominator in the life of every true Christian hero is faith. Where men have faith, they can reject pragmatism and embrace principle. Where they have faith, they can dare great deeds for the glory of God. This principle is beautifully communicated in the eleventh chapter of the Book of Hebrews. There we learn that God often raises up men to be standard-bearers for truth, even at the cost of their own lives.

The following chapter highlights some of the more inspirational verses about men who acted with courage and faith when it really mattered. Included is the heroic war cry of King Alfred, the thrilling account of the patriot pastors of 1776 who left the pulpit—rifle in hand—to defend their homes, and a tribute to the men of the *Titanic* who gladly gave up their lifeboat seats for women and children.

Faith and Warfare ❧

A Battle Hymn

Forth to the battle rides our King; He climbs His conquering car;
He fits His arrows to the string, and hurls His bolts afar.
Convictions pierce the stoutest hearts, they smart, they bleed, they die;
Slain by Immanuel's well-aimed darts, in helpless heaps they lie.

Behold, He bares His two-edged sword, and deals almighty blows;
His all-revealing, killing Word 'twixt joints and marrow goes.
Who can resist Him in the fight? He cuts through coats of mail.
Before the terror of His might the hearts of rebels fail.

Anon, arrayed in robes of grace, he rides the trampled plain,
With pity beaming in His face, and mercy in His train.
Mighty to save He now appears, mighty to raise the dead,
Mighty to staunch the bleeding wound, and lift the fallen head.

Victor alike in love and arms, myriads around Him bend;
Each captive owns His matchless charms, each foe becomes His friend.
They crown Him on the battle-field, they press to kiss His feet;
Their hands, their hearts, their all they yield: His conquest is complete.

None love Him more than those He slew; His love their hate has slain;
Henceforth their souls are all on fire to spread His gentle reign.

Charles H. Spurgeon

❧

THE PATRIOT PASTOR, *or*
THE RISING IN 1776

Out of the North, the wild news came,
Far flashing on its wings of fame,
Swift as the boreal light which flies
At midnight through the startled skies.
And there was tumult in the air,
The fife's shrill note, the drum's loud beat,
And through the wide land everywhere
The answering tread of hurrying feet;
While the first oath of Freedom's gun
Came on the blast from Lexington;
And Concord, roused, no longer tame,
Forgot her old baptismal name,
Made bare her patriot arm of power,
And swelled the discord of the hour.

Within its shade of elm and oak
The church of Berkely Manor stood;
There Sunday found the rural folk,
And some esteemed of gentle blood.
In vain their feet with loitering tread
Passed 'mid the graves where ran is naught;
All could not read the lesson taught
In that republic of the dead.
How sweet the hour of Sabbath talk,
The vale with peace and sunshine full
Where all the happy people walk,
Decked in their homespun flax and wool!
Where youth's gay hats with blossoms bloom;
And every maid with simple art,
Wears on her breast, like her own heart,
A bud whose depths are all perfume;

While every garment's gentle stir
Is breathing rose and lavender.

The pastor came; his snowy locks
Hallowed his brow of thought and care;
And calmly, as shepherds lead their flocks,
He led into the house of prayer.
The pastor rose; the prayer was strong;
The psalm was warrior's David's song;
The text, a few short words of might—
"The Lord of hosts shall arm the right!"

He spoke of wrongs too long endured,
Of sacred rights to be secured;
Then from his patriot tongue of flame
The startling words from Freedom came.
The stirring sentences he spake
Compelled the heart to glow or quake,
And, rising on his theme's broad wing,
And grasping in his nervous hand
The imaginary battle brand,
In face of death he dared to fling
Defiance to a tyrant king.

Even as he spoke, his frame, renewed
In eloquence of attitude,
Rose, as it seemed, a shoulder higher;
Then swept his kindling glance of fire
From startling pew to breathless choir;
When suddenly his mantle wide
His hands impatient flung aside,
And, lo, he met their wondering eyes
Complete in all a warrior's guise.

A moment there was awful pause,—
When Berkely cried, "Cease, traitor! Cease!
God's temple is the house of peace!"
The others shouted, "Nay, not so,
When God is with our righteous cause;
His holiest places then are ours,
His temples are our forts and towers,
That frown upon the tyrant foe;
In this, the dawn of Freedom's day,
There is a time to fight and pray!"

And now before the open door—
The warrior priest had ordered so—
The enlisting trumpet's sudden roar
Rang through the chapel, o'er and o'er,
Its long and reverberating blow.
So loud and clear, it seemed the ear
Of dusty death must wake and hear.

And there the startling drum and fife
Fired the living with fiercer life;
While overhead, with wild increase,
Forgetting its ancient toll of peace,
The great bell swung as ne'er before:
It seemed as it would never cease;
And every word its ardor flung
From off its jubilant iron tongue
Was, "War! War! War!"

"Who dares?"—This was the patriot's cry,
As striding from the desk he came,—
"Come out with me, in Freedom's name,
For her to live, for her to die?"

A hundred hands flung up reply,
A hundred voices answered, "I!"

Thomas Buchanan Read

৯়

RISE UP, O MEN OF GOD

Rise up, O men of God!
Have done with lesser things.
Give heart and mind and soul and strength
To serve the King of kings.

Rise up, O men of God!
The kingdom tarries long.
Bring in the day of brotherhood
And end the night of wrong.

Rise up, O men of God!
The Church for you doth wait,
Her strength unequal to her task;
Rise up, and make her great!

Lift high the cross of Christ!
Tread where His feet have trod.
As brothers of the Son of Man,
Rise up, O men of God!

৯়

KING ALFRED'S WAR SONG

When the enemy comes in a'roarin' like a flood,
Coveting the kingdom and hungering for blood,
The Lord will raise a standard up and lead His people on,
The Lord of Hosts will go before defeating every foe;
 defeating every foe.

For the Lord is our defense, Jesus defend us,
For the Lord is our defense, Jesu defend.

Some men trust in chariots, some trust in the horse,
But we will depend upon the Name of Christ our Lord,
The Lord has made my hands to war and my fingers to fight.
The Lord lays low our enemies, but He raises us upright;
 He raises us upright.

For the Lord is our defense, Jesus defend us,
For the Lord is our defense, Jesu defend.

A thousand fall on my left hand, ten thousand to the right,
But He will defend us from the arrow in the night.
Protect us from the terrors of the teeth of the devourer,
Embue us with your Spirit, Lord, encompass us with power;
 encompass us with power.

For the Lord is our defense, Jesus defend us,
For the Lord is our defense, Jesu defend.

ॐ

Chivalry and Sacrifice ❧

WOMEN AND CHILDREN FIRST

I.

The North Atlantic icefields are perilous and rough,
And only should be tested by those of sterner stuff;
They're filled with fearful hazards for nautical machines—
Icebergs that look like mountains, with jagged peaks and mean.

But on this eve in 1912, a monarch of the sea
Traversed her waves with brazen strides amid a night of glee.
"Unsinkable!" they called her, yes, unsinkable, their claim;
But pride, not strength, would give this ship a destiny of fame.

Near half a hundred thousand tons—the largest ship at sea!
A mighty maiden of the waves, in length: eight eighty-three.
A monument to science? No, a legacy of pride.
A testimonial to those who needlessly would die.

II.

While children's heads lay nestled warm and snug through
    midnight hours,
And husbands huddled next to wives asleep in love's sweet powers,
In upper decks men smoked and sang and toasted with a drink,
Not knowing that the virgin ship would soon begin to sink.

First rang the bells, then came the cries, and last the dreaded panic,
And now all knew t'would be the end of R.M.S. *Titanic*.
But in that hour of foul despair and fear unmitigated
A manly Christian cry to all was quickly circulated:

"Women and children first," they cried,
"Women and children first!
To save your souls you must give your lives,
Women and children first!"

III.

Amidst the tumult and the toil of lives then gripped with fear,
A holy calm prevailed on those whose hearts and minds were clear;
The cause was right, the mission pure, the path uncompromised;
The men must die that others live—the men must give their lives.

No greater love hath any man than that he lay down life
For family: for little ones, for dearest bride and wife.
What manly breast would shirk the call, or fail with any breath
To give his life for womankind, a sacrifice of death.

"Women and children first," the cry,
"Women and children first!"
Some must live while others die;
"Women and children first!"

IV.

As water surged upon the decks and chaos reigned supreme,
The band played on sweet hymns to God, which quieted the screams.
Some raised their hands, or cried aloud, while others genuflected,
In fleeting hopes that dreams and lives might still be resurrected.

Across the deck a thousand scenes of lives held in the balance,
With prayers delivered unto God in heavenly reliance.
While stokers, stewards, officers, and gentlemen en masse
All lifted women into boats without regard to class.

Women and children first—the law!
Women and children first.
The men would act—No fight. No flaw.
Women and children first.

V.

One faithful father searched the deck to find his family,
And rushing forward grabbed a girl near tossed into the sea.
But though this little golden hair was to the man a stranger,
He strapped to her his own life vest to save the babe from danger.

At last he saw the face he loved and pulled her from the throng,
Along with tender tiny ones who thought him bold and strong.
A little boy, a little girl—the world he held so dear,
Were waiting ignorant that time would bring their darkest fear.

Women and children first-praise God!
Women and children first.
This principle we ever laud!
Women and children first.

VI.

Five minutes he had to say goodbye, five minutes then all was lost,
But giving his life for the woman he loved was hardly a weighty cost.
"To the boats! To the boats, my darlings," said he, "to the boats!"
    and his words did race,
Then low'ring them into those cradles of life, he paused . . . just
    one more embrace.

And now he kissed those tender lips, and now he squeezed the hands,
And now he hugged and spoke the last of love and wedding bands.
"Be brave my love. Be brave my son. Be brave my little dears.
God's ways are just, Christ rules above, and faith must hush our fears."

"Women and children first," said he,
"Women and children first;
To be a man I must set you free.
Women and children first!"

VII.

At last he said goodbye to eyes which longed for him and home,
At last he watched them pull away to safety through the foam,
In moments he would be submerged and 'neath the icy brine,
Content to know his sacrifice had given them more time.

Just yards away a mother gazed back at the sinking boat,
Her children bundled in her arms, warmed by their mother's coat.
A prayer of hope upon her lips, a Bible in her hand,
A testament of love, of faith, and of her husband's stand.

"Women and children first," she wept.
"Women and children first,"
Stroking the curls of the infant she'd kept,
"Women and children first."

VIII.

Into the liquid tomb he fell, moments from paradise,
With one last grasp he clawed the waves and caught his dear one's eyes.
His frozen face, his numb-ed hands, his body stiff and cold —
An ocean legacy of heroism told.

Down through the depths *Titanic* sank, and into her watery grave,
Bound by such forces that God had decreed would render the hulk
    its slave.
Downward she plunged through the darkness so cold, taking no
    inventory
Of perishing hundreds who crowded her decks, bound for Hell or
    Glory.

For women and children first they died,
For women and children first;
They put their faith before their pride,
For women and children first.

Douglas W. Phillips
dedicated on April 15, 1997
at the Titanic *Men's Memorial*

❦

HOW DID YOU DIE?

Did you tackle that trouble that came your way
With a resolute heart and cheerful?
Or hide your face from the light of day
With a craven soul and fearful?
Oh, a trouble's a ton, or a trouble's an ounce,
Or a trouble is what you make it,
And it isn't the fact that you're hurt that counts,
But only how did you take it?

You are beaten to earth? Well, well, what's that?
Come up with a smiling face.
It's nothing against you to fall down flat,
But to lie there—that's disgrace.
The harder you're thrown, why the higher you bounce;
Be proud of your blackened eye!
It isn't the fact that you're licked that counts,
It's how did you fight—and why?

And though you be done to the death, what then?
If you battled the best you could,
If you played your part in the world of men,
Why, the Critic will call it good.
Death comes with a crawl, or comes with a pounce,
And whether he's slow or spry,
It isn't the fact that you're dead that counts,
But only how did you die?

Edmund Vance Cooke

Duty and Honor ❧

GIVE US MEN

Give us Men!
Men—from every rank,
Fresh and free and frank;
Men of thought and reading,
Men of light and leading,
Men of loyal breeding,
The nation's welfare speeding;
Men of faith and not of fiction,
Men of lofty aim in action;
Give us Men—O say again,
Give us Men!

Give us Men!
Strong and stalwart ones;
Men whom purest honor fires,
Men who trample self beneath them,
Men who make their country wreathe them
As her noble sons,
Worthy of their sires;
Men who never shame their mothers,
Men who never fail their brothers,
True, however false are others:
Give us Men—I say again,
Give us Men!

Give us Men!
Men who, when tempest gathers,
Grasp the standard of their fathers
In the thickest fight;
Men who strike for home and altar,
(Let the coward cringe and falter),
God defend the right!
True as truth the lorn and lonely,
Tender, as the brave are only;
Men who tread where saints have trod,
Men for Country, Home—and God:
Give us Men! I say again—again—
Give us Men!

Josiah Gilbert Holland

❧

"We Few, We Happy Few, We Band of Brothers"
St. Crispin's Day Speech

Westmoreland
O that we now had here
But one ten thousand of those men in England
That do no work to-day!

King Henry
What's he that wishes so?
My cousin Westmoreland? No, my fair cousin;
If we are mark'd to die, we are enough
To do our country loss; and if to live,
The fewer men, the greater share of honour.

God's will! I pray thee, wish not one man more.
By Jove, I am not covetous for gold,
Nor care I who doth feed upon my cost;
It yearns me not if men my garments wear;
Such outward things dwell not in my desires.
But if it be a sin to covet honour,
I am the most offending soul alive.

No, faith, my coz, wish not a man from England.
God's peace! I would not lose so great an honour
As one man more methinks would share from me
For the best hope I have. O, do not wish one more!
Rather proclaim it, Westmoreland, through my host,
That he which hath no stomach to this fight,
Let him depart; his passport shall be made,
And crowns for convoy put into his purse;

We would not die in that man's company
That fears his fellowship to die with us.

This day is call'd the feast of Crispian.
He that outlives this day, and comes safe home,
Will stand a tip-toe when this day is nam'd,
And rouse him at the name of Crispian.

He that shall live this day, and see old age,
Will yearly on the vigil feast his neighbours,
And say "To-morrow is Saint Crispian."
Then will he strip his sleeve and show his scars,
And say "These wounds I had on Crispian's day."

Old men forget; yet all shall be forgot,
But he'll remember, with advantages,
What feats he did that day. Then shall our names,
Familiar in his mouth as household words—
Harry the King, Bedford and Exeter,
Warwick and Talbot, Salisbury and Gloucester—
Be in their flowing cups freshly rememb'red.

This story shall the good man teach his son;
And Crispin Crispian shall ne'er go by,
From this day to the ending of the world,
But we in it shall be remembered—
We few, we happy few, we band of brothers;
For he to-day that sheds his blood with me
Shall be my brother; be he ne'er so vile,
This day shall gentle his condition;
And gentlemen in England now-a-bed
Shall think themselves accurs'd they were not here,
And hold their manhoods cheap whiles any speaks
That fought with us upon Saint Crispin's day.

From "Henry V" by William Shakespeare

The Charge of the Light Brigade

Half a league, half a league,
   Half a league onward,
All in the valley of Death
   Rode the six hundred.
"Forward, the Light Brigade!
Charge for the guns!" he said:
Into the valley of Death
   Rode the six hundred.

"Forward, the Light Brigade!"
Was there a man dismay'd?
Not tho' the soldier knew
   Someone had blunder'd:
Their's not to make reply,
Their's not to reason why,
Their's but to do and die:
Into the valley of Death
   Rode the six hundred.

Cannon to right of them,
Cannon to left of them,
Cannon in front of them
   Volley'd and thunder'd;
Storm'd at with shot and shell,
Boldly they rode and well,
Into the jaws of Death,
Into the mouth of Hell
   Rode the six hundred.

Flash'd all their sabres bare,
Flash'd as they turn'd in air,
Sabring the gunners there,
Charging an army, while
 All the world wonder'd:
Plunged in the battery-smoke
Right thro' the line they broke;
Cossack and Russian
Reel'd from the sabre stroke
 Shatter'd and sunder'd.
Then they rode back, but not
 Not the six hundred.

Cannon to right of them,
Cannon to left of them,
Cannon behind them
 Volley'd and thunder'd;
Storm'd at with shot and shell,
While horse and hero fell,
They that had fought so well
Came thro' the jaws of Death
Back from the mouth of Hell,
All that was left of them,
 Left of six hundred.

When can their glory fade?
O the wild charge they made!
 All the world wondered.
Honor the charge they made,
Honor the Light Brigade,
 Noble six hundred.

Alfred Lord Tennyson

Command and Leadership ❧

Stonewall Jackson's Way

Come, stack arms, men! pile on the rails,
Stir up the camp-fire bright;
No growling if the canteen fails,
We'll make a roaring night.
Here Shenandoah brawls along,
There burly Blue Ridge echoes strong,
To swell the Brigade's rousing song
Of "Stonewall Jackson's way."

We see him now—the queer slouched hat
Cocked o'er his eye askew;
The shrewd, dry smile; the speech so pat,
So calm, so blunt, so true.
The "Blue-light Elder" knows 'em well;
Says he, "That's Banks—he's fond of shell;
Lord save his soul! we'll give him"—well!
That's "Stonewall Jackson's way."

Silence! ground arms! kneel all! caps off
Old Massa's goin' to pray.
Strangle the fool that dares to scoff
Attention! it's his way.
Appealing from his native sod
In *forma pauperis* to God:
"Lay bare Thine arm; stretch forth Thy rod!
Amen!" That's "Stonewall's way."

He's in the saddle now. Fall in!
Steady! the whole brigade!
Hill's at the ford, cut off; we'll win
His way out, ball and blade!
What matter if our shoes are worn?
What matter if our feet are torn?
"Quick step! we're with him before morn!"
That's "Stonewall Jackson's way."

The sun's bright lances rout the mists
Of morning, and, by George!
Here's Longstreet, struggling in the lists,
Hemmed in an ugly gorge.
Pope and his Dutchmen, whipped before;
"Bay'nets and grape!" hear Stonewall roar;
"Charge, Stuart! Pay off Ashby's score"
In "Stonewall Jackson's way."

Ah, Maiden! wait and watch and yearn
For news of Stonewall's band,
Ah, widow! read, with eyes that burn,
That ring upon thy hand,
Ah, Wife! sew on, pray on, hope on;
Thy life shall not be all forlorn;
The foe had better ne'er been born
That gets in "Stonewall's way."

John Williamson Palmer, 1862

Principle and Perseverance ❧

ONCE TO EVERY MAN AND NATION

Once to every man and nation comes the moment to decide,
In the strife of truth and falsehood, for the good or evil side;
Some great cause, some great decision, diff'ring each the bloom or blight,
And the choice goes by forever 'twixt that darkness and that light.

Then to side with truth is noble, when we share her wretched crust,
Ere her cause bring fame and profit, and 'tis prosp'rous to be just;
Then it is the brave man chooses while the coward stands aside,
Till the multitude make virtue of the faith they had denied.

Though the cause of evil prosper, yet the truth alone is strong;
Though her portion be the scaffold, and upon the throne be wrong,
Yet that scaffold sways the future, and behind the dim unknown,
Standeth God within the shadow keeping watch above His own.

James R. Lowell

❧

ODE TO DABNEY

In addition to his role as personal assistant to Stonewall Jackson, Robert Louis Dabney is best know as the premier defender of Christian orthodoxy to emerge from the South in the latter half of the 19th century. A theologian of rock-solid convictions, Dabney not only stood against the rising tide of modernity, but he was able to predict with devastating accuracy the consequences of compromise for the American church.

We must remember Thornwell, Palmer, Girardeau—
All Southern men who preached with power, unity, and flow;
But when it comes to logic pure there's one that tops our list:
Hail Dabney, prophet of the South, our great apologist.

Geneva had its Calvin, Rome its Augustine,
England had is Cromwell to fight the libertine;
But in our land there was but one who dared to turn the tide
Of reconstructionistic zeal and yankeedom's foul pride.

The feminist, the plutocrat, the wiley carpetbagger,
The Darwinist, the bureaucrat, and transcendental braggart;
The scalawag, the suffragette, the surly Statist simp
Were by your pen defrocked, exposed, and wounded, left to limp.

The solomonic wisdom from your pugilistic pen
Has rendered impotent the creeds of far less noble men;
And with a keen, perceptive flair that exceeds Nostradamus,
Your prophesies have proven wrong each foolish doubting Thomas.

You make us leave our comfort zone and re-engage the battle,
Content no more to tolerate the sophomoric prattle
Of Socialists, Republicrats, and those who compromise;
No longer may we coddle them or listen to their lies.

And so with joy we doff our hats and shout from every mouth:
Hail Dabney, wise apologist, defender of the South!

Douglas W. Phillips

❧

Somebody Said It Couldn't Be Done

Somebody said that it couldn't be done
But he with a chuckle replied
That "maybe it couldn't," but he would be one
Who wouldn't say so till he tried.
So he buckled right in with the trace of a grin
On his face. If he worried he hid it.
He started to sing as he tackled the thing
That couldn't be done, and he did it!

Somebody scoffed: "Oh, you'll never do that;
At least no one ever has done it;"
But he took off his coat and he took off his hat
And the first thing we knew he'd begun it.
With a lift of his chin and a bit of a grin,
Without any doubting or quiddit,
He started to sing as he tackled the thing
That couldn't be done, and he did it.

There are thousands to tell you it cannot be done,
There are thousands to prophesy failure,
There are thousands to point out to you one by one,
The dangers that wait to assail you.
But just buckle in with a bit of a grin,
Just take off your coat and go to it;
Just start in to sing as you tackle the thing
That "cannot be done," and you'll do it.

When you're up against a trouble,
Meet it squarely, face to face;
Lift your chin and set your shoulders,
Plant your feet and take a brace.
When it's vain to try to dodge it,
Do the best that you can do;
You may fail, but you may conquer,
See it through!

Black may be the clouds about you
And your future may seem grim,
But don't let your nerve desert you;
Keep yourself in fighting trim.
If the worst is bound to happen,
Spite of all that you can do,
Running from it will not save you,
See it through!

Edgar Guest

୬

If

If you can keep your head when all about you
Are losing theirs and blaming it on you,
If you can trust yourself when all men doubt you,
But make allowance for their doubting too;
If you can wait and not be tired by waiting,
Or being lied about, don't deal in lies,
Or being hated don't give way to hating,
And yet don't look too good, nor talk too wise:

If you can dream—and not make dreams your master;
If you can think—and not make thoughts your aim;
If you can meet with Triumph and Disaster
And treat those two impostors just the same;
If you can bear to hear the truth you've spoken
Twisted by knaves to make a trap for fools,
Or watch the things you gave your life to, broken,
And stoop and build 'em up with worn-out tools:

If you can make one heap of all your winnings
And risk it on one turn of pitch-and-toss,
And lose, and start again at your beginnings
And never breathe a word about your loss;
If you can force your heart and nerve and sinew
To serve your turn long after they are gone,
And so hold on when there is nothing in you
Except the Will which says to them: "Hold on!"

If you can talk with crowds and keep your virtue,
Or walk with Kings—nor lose the common touch,
If neither foes nor loving friends can hurt you,
If all men count with you, but none too much;
If you can fill the unforgiving minute
With sixty seconds' worth of distance run,
Yours is the Earth and everything that's in it,
And—which is more—you'll be a Man, my son!

Rudyard Kipling

POEMS OF
PATRIOTISM

Give ear, O my people, to my law: incline your ears to the words of my mouth. I will open my mouth in a parable: I will utter dark sayings of old: Which we have heard and known, and our fathers have told us. We will not hide them from their children, Shewing to the generation to come the praises of the LORD, And His strength, and His wonderful works that He hath done. For He established a testimony in Jacob, and appointed a law in Israel, Which he commanded our fathers, that they should make them known to their children: That the generation to come might know them, Even the children which should be born; Who should arise and declare them to their children; That they might set their hope in God, And not forget the works of God, but keep his commandments; And might not be as their fathers, a stubborn and rebellious generation; A generation that set not their heart aright, And whose spirit was not steadfast with God.

PSALM 78

Patriotism

The word "patriotism" means love of and devotion to one's country. However, the biblical doctrine of patriotism is not rooted in modern notions of blind jingoistic sentiment, but rather on the fact that the Bible teaches that God Himself has ordained national boundaries, that He has established rulers and governments, that we are to show appreciation and respect to such, and that He places every man in the context of a national identity.

In fact, the Bible not only teaches that men are to be understood as part of "tribes and tongues and nations," but that there is a sense in which Christians may enjoy the privilege of dual citizenship. Our first citizenship is in Heaven, but like the Apostle Paul, we may boldly stand on the earthly citizenship God has given us.

Patriotism is, therefore, a duty before God. It is the holy obligation of all Christian men to give thanks for their country. They do so by remembering the mighty deeds of God in that country, by working for righteousness in the land, and by urging repentance when the nation transgresses His laws. Furthermore, there is an important link between patriotism and patriarchy. The patriarch seeks to build a multi-generational legacy of faithfulness. This message is communicated to children by giving them an historical context for the work of Christ in the life of their family. Our founding fathers, most of whom were fourth-generation descendants of the original settlers, understood this principle, and constantly harkened back to the first fathers through whom God laid the foundations of liberty.

Love of Country ❧

BREATHES THERE THE MAN

To be anti-patriotic is to be a spiritual ingrate. Where God has prospered a nation, the people of God must rise up and bless His holy name. That is why it is the height of ingratitude to Almighty God to take one's nation for granted. Love of country is one of the great loves that defines the heart of the patriarch. Scott eloquently communicates this principle in this brief but devastating poem.

Breathes there the man, with soul so dead,
Who never to himself hath said,
"This is my own, my native land!"
Whose heart hath ne'er within him burned,
As home his footsteps he hath turned,
From wandering on a foreign strand!

If such there breathe, go, mark him well;
For him no Minstrel raptures swell;
High though his titles, proud his name,
Boundless his wealth as wish can claim;
Despite those titles, power, and pelf,
The wretch, concerned all in self,
Living, shall forfeit fair renown,
And, doubly dying, shall go down
To the vile dust, from whence he sprung,
Unwept, unhonored, and unsung.

Sir Walter Scott

❧

AMERICA THE BEAUTIFUL

Katharine Lee Bates wrote the original version of "America the Beautiful" in 1893, the second version in 1904, and the final version in 1913. She once commented: "One day some of the other teachers and I decided to go on a trip to 14,000-foot Pikes Peak. We hired a prairie wagon. Near the top we had to leave the wagon and go the rest of the way on mules. I was very tired. But when I saw the view, I felt great joy. All the wonder of America seemed displayed there, with the sea-like expanse."

AMERICA THE BEAUTIFUL—1913

O beautiful for spacious skies,
For amber waves of grain,
For purple mountain majesties
Above the fruited plain!
America! America!
God shed his grace on thee
And crown thy good with brotherhood
From sea to shining sea!

O beautiful for pilgrim feet
Whose stern, impassioned stress
A thoroughfare for freedom beat
Across the wilderness!
America! America!
God mend thine every flaw,
Confirm thy soul in self-control,
Thy liberty in law!

O beautiful for heroes proved
In liberating strife.
Who more than self thy country loved
And mercy more than life!
America! America!
May God thy gold refine
Till all success be nobleness
And every gain divine!

O beautiful for patriot dream
That sees beyond the years
Thine alabaster cities gleam
Undimmed by human tears!
America! America!
God shed his grace on thee
And crown thy good with brotherhood
From sea to shining sea!

O beautiful for halcyon skies,
For amber waves of grain,
For purple mountain majesties
Above the enameled plain!
America! America!
God shed his grace on thee
Till souls wax fair as earth and air
And music-hearted sea!

O beautiful for pilgrims' feet,
Whose stern impassioned stress
A thoroughfare for freedom beat
Across the wilderness!
America! America!
God shed his grace on thee
Till paths be wrought through
Wilds of thought
By pilgrim foot and knee!

O beautiful for glory-tale
Of liberating strife
When once and twice,
For man's avail
Men lavished precious life!
America! America!
God shed his grace on thee
Till selfish gain no longer stain
The banner of the free!

O beautiful for patriot dream
That sees beyond the years
Thine alabaster cities gleam
Undimmed by human tears!
America! America!
God shed his grace on thee
Till nobler men keep once again
Thy whiter jubilee!

Katharine Lee Bates

Our Forefather's Legacy ❧

THE LANDING OF THE PILGRIM FATHERS

The breaking waves dashed high
On a stern and rock-bound coast,
And the woods, against a stormy sky,
Their giant branches tossed;
And the heavy night hung dark
The hills and waters o'er,
When a band of exiles moored their bark
On a wild New England shore.

Not as the conqueror comes,
They, the true-hearted, came;
Not with the roll of the stirring drums,
And the trumpet that sings of fame;
Not as the flying come,
In silence and in fear;
They shook the depths of the desert's gloom
With their hymns of lofty cheer.

Amidst the storm they sang,
And the stars heard, and the sea;
And the sounding aisles of the dim woods rang
To the anthem of the free!
The ocean-eagle soared
From his nest by the white wave's foam,
And the rocking pines of the forest roared;
This was their welcome home!

There were men with hoary hair
Amidst that pilgrim band;
Why had they come to wither there,
Away from their childhood's land?
There was woman's fearless eye,
Lit by her deep love's truth;
There was manhood's brow, serenely high,
And the fiery heart of youth.

What sought they thus afar?
Bright jewels of the mine?
The wealth of seas, the spoils of war?
They sought a faith's pure shrine!
Aye, call it holy ground,
The soil where they first trod!
They left unstained what there they found—
Freedom to worship God!

Felicia Dorthea Hemans

ॐ

PAUL REVERE'S RIDE

Listen, my children, and you shall hear
Of the midnight ride of Paul Revere,
On the eighteenth of April, in Seventy-five;
Hardly a man is now alive
Who remembers that famous day and year.
He said to his friend, "If the British march
By land or sea from the town to-night,
Hang a lantern aloft in the belfry arch
Of the North Church tower as a signal light,—
One if by land, and two if by sea;

And I on the opposite shore will be,
Ready to ride and spread the alarm
Through every Middlesex village and farm,
For the country folk to be up and to arm."

Then he said "Good-night!" and with muffled oar
Silently rowed to the Charlestown shore,
Just as the moon rose over the bay,
Where swinging wide at her moorings lay
The *Somerset*, British man-of-war;
A phantom ship, with each mast and spar
Across the moon like a prison bar,
And a huge black hulk, that was magnified
By its own reflection in the tide.
Meanwhile, his friend through alley and street
Wanders and watches, with eager ears,
Till in the silence around him he hears
The muster of men at the barrack door,
The sound of arms, and the tramp of feet,
And the measured tread of the grenadiers,
Marching down to their boats on the shore.

Then he climbed the tower of the Old North Church,
By the wooden stairs, with stealthy tread,
To the belfry chamber overhead,
And startled the pigeons from their perch
On the sombre rafters, that round him made
Masses and moving shapes of shade,—
By the trembling ladder, steep and tall,
To the highest window in the wall,
Where he paused to listen and look down
A moment on the roofs of the town
And the moonlight flowing over all.
Beneath, in the churchyard, lay the dead,

In their night encampment on the hill,
Wrapped in silence so deep and still
That he could hear, like a sentinel's tread,
The watchful night-wind, as it went
Creeping along from tent to tent,
And seeming to whisper, "All is well!"

A moment only he feels the spell
Of the place and the hour, and the secret dread
Of the lonely belfry and the dead;
For suddenly all his thoughts are bent
On a shadowy something far away,
Where the river widens to meet the bay,—
A line of black that bends and floats
On the rising tide like a bridge of boats.
Meanwhile, impatient to mount and ride,
Booted and spurred, with a heavy stride
On the opposite shore walked Paul Revere.
Now he patted his horse's side,
Now he gazed at the landscape far and near,
Then, impetuous, stamped the earth,
And turned and tightened his saddle girth;
But mostly he watched with eager search
The belfry tower of the Old North Church,
As it rose above the graves on the hill,
Lonely and spectral and sombre and still.
And lo! as he looks, on the belfry's height
A glimmer, and then a gleam of light!
He springs to the saddle, the bridle he turns,
But lingers and gazes, till full on his sight
A second lamp in the belfry burns.
A hurry of hoofs in a village street,
A shape in the moonlight, a bulk in the dark,
And beneath, from the pebbles, in passing, a spark

Struck out by a steed flying fearless and fleet;
That was all! And yet, through the gloom and the light,
The fate of a nation was riding that night;
And the spark struck out by that steed, in his flight,
Kindled the land into flame with its heat.
He has left the village and mounted the steep,
And beneath him, tranquil and broad and deep,
Is the Mystic, meeting the ocean tides;
And under the alders that skirt its edge,
Now soft on the sand, now loud on the ledge,
Is heard the tramp of his steed as he rides.
It was twelve by the village clock
When he crossed the bridge into Medford town.
He heard the crowing of the cock,
And the barking of the farmer's dog,
And felt the damp of the river fog,
That rises after the sun goes down.
It was one by the village clock,
When he galloped into Lexington.
He saw the gilded weathercock
Swim in the moonlight as he passed,
And the meeting-house windows, black and bare,
Gaze at him with a spectral glare,
As if they already stood aghast
At the bloody work they would look upon.
It was two by the village clock,
When he came to the bridge in Concord town.
He heard the bleating of the flock,
And the twitter of birds among the trees,
And felt the breath of the morning breeze
Blowing over the meadow brown.
And one was safe and asleep in his bed
Who at the bridge would be first to fall,

Who that day would be lying dead,
Pierced by a British musket ball.

You know the rest. In the books you have read
How the British Regulars fired and fled,
How the farmers gave them ball for ball,
From behind each fence and farmyard wall,
Chasing the redcoats down the lane,
Then crossing the fields to emerge again
Under the trees at the turn of the road,
And only pausing to fire and load.
So through the night rode Paul Revere;
And so through the night went his cry of alarm
To every Middlesex village and farm,
A cry of defiance, and not of fear,
A voice in the darkness, a knock at the door,
And a word that shall echo for evermore!
For, borne on the night-wind of the Past,
Through all our history, to the last,
In the hour of darkness and peril and need,
The people will waken and listen to hear
The hurrying hoof-beats of that steed,
And the midnight message of Paul Revere.

Henry Wadsworth Longfellow

৯৫

THE STAR SPANGLED BANNER

Oh, say can you see by the dawn's early light
What so proudly we hailed at the twilight's last gleaming?
Whose broad stripes and bright stars through the perilous fight,
O'er the ramparts we watched were so gallantly streaming?
And the rocket's red glare, the bombs bursting in air,
Gave proof through the night that our flag was still there.
Oh, say does that star-spangled banner yet wave
O'er the land of the free and the home of the brave?

On the shore, dimly seen through the mists of the deep,
Where the foe's haughty host in dread silence reposes,
What is that which the breeze, o'er the towering steep,
As it fitfully blows, half conceals, half discloses?
Now it catches the gleam of the morning's first beam,
In full glory reflected now shines in the stream:
'Tis the star-spangled banner! Oh long may it wave
O'er the land of the free and the home of the brave!

And where is that band who so vauntingly swore
That the havoc of war and the battle's confusion,
A home and a country should leave us no more!
Their blood has washed out their foul footsteps' pollution.
No refuge could save the hireling and slave
From the terror of flight, or the gloom of the grave:
And the star-spangled banner in triumph doth wave
O'er the land of the free and the home of the brave!

Oh! thus be it ever, when freemen shall stand
Between their loved home and the war's desolation!
Blest with victory and peace, may the heav'n rescued land
Praise the Power that hath made and preserved us a nation.
Then conquer we must, when our cause it is just,
And this be our motto: "In God is our trust."
And the star-spangled banner in triumph shall wave
O'er the land of the free and the home of the brave!

Francis Scott Key

Humility Before Almighty God ❧

RECESSIONAL

God of our fathers, known of old—
Lord of our far-flung battle line—
Beneath whose awful hand we hold
Dominion over palm and pine—
Lord God of Hosts, be with us yet,
Lest we forget—lest we forget!!

The tumult and the shouting dies—
The Captains and the Kings depart—
Still stands Thine ancient sacrifice,
An humble and a contrite heart.
Lord God of Hosts, be with us yet,
Lest we forget—lest we forget!!

Far-called our navies melt away—
On dune and headland sinks the fire—
Lo, all our pomp of yesterday
Is one with Nineveh and Tyre!
Judge of the Nations, spare us yet,
Lest we forget—lest we forget!!

If, drunk with sight of power, we loose
Wild tongues that have not Thee in awe—
Such boastings as the Gentiles use,
Or lesser breeds without the Law—
Lord God of Hosts, be with us yet,
Lest we forget—lest we forget!!

For heathen heart that puts her trust
In reeking tube and iron shard—
All valiant dust that builds on dust,
And guarding calls not Thee to guard.
For frantic boast and foolish word,
Thy Mercy on Thy People, Lord!

Amen.

Rudyard Kipling

Poems for the Children's Hour

But Jesus said, Suffer little children, and forbid them not, to come unto me: for of such is the kingdom of heaven.

MATTHEW 19:14

Blessed is every one that feareth the LORD; that walketh in his ways. For thou shalt eat the labour of thine hands: Happy shalt thou be, and it shall be well with thee. Thy wife shall be as a fruitful vine by the sides of thine house; Thy children like olive plants round about thy table. Behold, that thus shall the man be blessed that feareth the LORD. The LORD shall bless thee out of Zion: And thou shalt see the good of Jerusalem all the days of thy life. Yea, thou shalt see thy children's children, and peace upon Israel.

PSALM 128

THE CHILDREN'S HOUR

The daily rituals of working with one's family, receiving both formal and informal instruction within the home, caring for other family members, reading aloud, and playing with brothers and sisters was once the hallmark of Christian family life in American culture. Much of this culture of Christian family life began to change in the 19th century with the impact of the industrial revolution on fatherhood, and the rise and the spirit of egalitarianism which transformed the family from a unity where each member drew strength from the whole, to a collection of individuals, each demanding rights and autonomy.

Nineteenth century poet Henry Wadsworth Longfellow was one of many commentators who observed this shift in family culture. Perhaps better than any other American poet of his generation, Longfellow was able to capture in verse the beauty of hearth and home. His classic poem, "The Children's Hour," communicates in the most sympathetic manner what it means to "suffer the children" to come unto their fathers. (Once during our family devotions, I surprised my children with the poem you are about to read. My children giggled, especially about the idea of sneaking up on Daddy in his study, because this is a common occurrence in our home.)

Oh fathers, may each of us take the time to suffer the children to come unto us. May we rejoice and delight in their golden curls, their sweet smiles, and their glorious giggles. May we never harm them through selfish indifference or misplaced priorities.

THE CHILDREN'S HOUR

Between the dark and the daylight,
When the night is beginning to lower,
Comes a pause in the day's occupations,
That is known as the Children's Hour.
I hear in the chamber above me
The patter of little feet,
The sound of a door that is opened,
And voices soft and sweet.

From my study I see in the lamplight,
Descending the broad hall stair,
Grave Alice, and laughing Allegra,
And Edith with golden hair.
A whisper, and then a silence:
Yet I know by their merry eyes
They are plotting and planning together
To take me by surprise.

A sudden rush from the stairway,
A sudden raid from the hall!
By three doors left unguarded
They enter my castle wall!
They climb up into my turret
O'er the arms and back of my chair;
If I try to escape, they surround me;
They seem to be everywhere.

They almost devour me with kisses,
Their arms about me entwine,
Till I think of the Bishop of Bingen
In his Mouse-Tower on the Rhine!
Do you think, O blue-eyed banditti,
Because you have scaled the wall,
Such an old mustache as I am
Is not a match for you all!

I have you fast in my fortress,
And will not let you depart,
But put you down into the dungeon
In the round-tower of my heart.
And there will I keep you forever,
Yes, forever and a day,
Till the walls shall crumble to ruin,
And moulder in dust away!

Henry Wadsworth Longfellow

❧

CHRIST AND THE LITTLE ONES

"The master has come over the Jordan,"
Said Hannah the mother one day;
"He is healing the people who throng Him,
With a touch of His finger, they say.

"And now I shall carry the children,
Little Rachel and Samuel and John,
I shall carry the baby Esther,
For the Lord to look upon."

The father looked at her kindly,
But he shook his head and smiled:
"Now who but a doting mother
Would think of a thing so wild?

"If the children were tortured by demons,
Or dying of fever, 'twere well;
Or had they the taint of the leper,
Like many in Israel."

"Nay, do not hinder me, Nathan,
I feel such a burden of care;
If I carry it to the Master,
Perhaps I shall leave it there.

"If He lay His hand on the children,
My heart will be lighter, I know,
For a blessing for ever and ever
Will follow them as they go."

So over the hills of Judah,
Along by the vine rows green,
With Esther asleep on her bosom,
And Rachel her brothers between;

'Mid the people who hung on His teaching,
Or waited His touch and His word,
Through the row of proud Pharisees listening
She pressed to the feet of the Lord.

"Now why should thou hinder the Master,"
Said Peter, "with children like these?
Seest not how from morning to evening
He teacheth and healeth disease?"

Then Christ said, "Forbid not the children,
Permit them to come unto me!"
And He took in His arms little Esther,
And Rachel He sat on His knee:

And the heavy heart of the mother
Was lifted all earth care above,
As He laid His hand on the brothers,
And blest them with holiest love;

As He said of the babes in His bosom,
"Of such are the kingdom of Heaven"—
And strength for all duty and trial
That hour to her spirit were given.

Julia Gill

❧

HOME, SWEET HOME

'Mid pleasures and palaces though we may roam,
Be it ever so humble, there's no place like home!
A charm from the skies seems to follow us there,
Which, seek through the world, is ne'er met with elsewhere.

Home, home! Sweet, sweet home!
Be it ever so humble, there's no place like home!

An exile from home, splendor dazzles in vain;
O, give me my lowly thatched cottage again!
The birds singing gaily, that come at my call:
Give me these, and the peace of mind dearer than all.

Home, home! Sweet, sweet home!
Be it ever so humble, there's no place like home!

John Howard Payne

POEMS OUR
FATHERS
TAUGHT US

O my people, hear my teaching; listen to the words of my mouth. I will open my mouth in parables, I will utter hidden things, things from of old—what we have heard and known, what our fathers have told us. We will not hide them from their children; we will tell the next generation the praiseworthy deeds of the LORD, his power, and the wonders he has done. He decreed statutes for Jacob and established the law in Israel, which he commanded our forefathers to teach their children, so the next generation would know them, even the children yet to be born, and they in turn would tell their children. Then they would put their trust in God and would not forget his deeds but would keep his commands.

PSALM 78

And all thy children shall be taught of the LORD; and great shall be the peace of thy children.

ISAIAH 54:23

Teaching Fathers

The Bible teaches that fathers, not school officials, and not even mothers, are to be the primary teachers of their children. Every command found in the Bible aimed at training, nurturing, and discipling children is first directed at fathers. What is more, the Bible says that teaching children "is not a vain thing . . . it is your life." (Deuteronomy 32:47).

The Lord reemphasized this principle during his earthly ministry. One day, Jesus was asked to name the greatest commandment. He quoted from the sixth chapter of Deuteronomy which reveals that loving God with all one's heart is the greatest commandment. That same passage makes it clear that the application of this commandment is for fathers to teach their children diligently—all the time. This principle is communicated throughout the Bible. Fathers are to be the resident historians, the primary educators, and yes, even the family poets, leading their households in verse and song before the Lord, which is why Psalm 78 (quoted at left) speaks of fathers teaching their children parables and "things from of old."

My personal experience sitting at hearth and table with my father as he read the classic works of poetry has remained with me my whole life, and is in part the inspiration for this volume. Included in this chapter are some of the great "father to son" poems which dads have been reading to their boys for the better part of a century.

The Village Blacksmith

To date, no one has surpassed Henry Wadsworth Longfellow in his ability to communicate what historian George Grant calls, "the nobility of the commonplace." Longfellow is truly America's poet, and "The Village Blacksmith" is quintessential Longfellow. Here we see manhood and patriarchy at its very best—rooted in honest labor, love of God, and the blessing of family life.

Under a spreading chestnut tree
The village smithy stands;
The smith, a mighty man is he,
With large and sinewy hands;
And the muscles of his brawny arms
Are strong as iron bands.

His hair is crisp, and black, and long,
His face is like the tan:
His brow is wet with honest sweat,
He earns whate'er he can,
And looks the whole world in the face,
For he owes not any man.

Week in, week out, from morn till night,
You can hear his bellows blow;
You can hear him swing his heavy sledge,
With measured beat and slow,
Like a sexton ringing the village bell,
When the evening sun is low.

And children coming home from school
Look in at the open door;
They love to see the flaming forge,

And hear the bellows roar,
And catch the burning sparks that fly
Life chaff from a threshing floor.

He goes on Sunday to the church,
And sits among his boys;
He hears the parson pray and preach,
He hears his daughter's voice,
Singing in the village choir,
And it makes his heart rejoice.

It sounds to him like her mother's voice,
Singing in Paradise!
He needs must think of her once more,
How in the grave she lies;
And with his hard, rough hand he wipes
A tear out of his eyes.

Toiling,—rejoicing,—sorrowing,
Onwards through life he goes;
Each morning sees some task begin,
Each evening sees it close;
Something attempted, something done,
Has earned a night's repose.

Thanks, thanks to thee, my worthy friend,
For the lesson thou hast taught!
Thus at the flaming forge of life
Our fortunes must be wrought;
Thus on its sounding anvil shaped
Each burning deed and thought!

Henry Wadsworth Longfellow

CASEY AT THE BAT

Since its first publication in 1888, generations of fathers have passed on the the story of Casey to their sons. In many respects it is the ultimate American poem. Although the context of the poem is our national pastime—baseball—"Casey" is really about the passion and poetry that Americans find in life. It is about the rise and fall of the hero and the fickleness of the crowd.

The Outlook wasn't brilliant for the Mudville nine that day:
The score stood four to two, with but one inning more to play.
And then when Cooney died at first, and Barrows did the same,
A sickly silence fell upon the patrons of the game.

A straggling few got up to go in deep despair. The rest
Clung to that hope which springs eternal in the human breast;
They thought, if only Casey could get but a whack at that—
We'd pit up even money, now, with Casey at the bat.

But Flynn preceded Casey, as did also Jimmy Blake,
And the former was a lulu and the latter was a fake;
So upon that stricken multitude from melancholy sat,
For there seemed but little chance of Casey's getting to the bat.

But Flynn let drive a single, to the wonderment of all,
And Blake, the much despis-ed, tore the cover off the ball;
And when the dust had lifted, and the men saw what had occurred,
There was Johnny safe at second and Flynn a-hugging third.

Then from five thousand throats and more there rose a lusty yell;
It rumbled through the valley, it rattled in the dell;
It knocked upon the mountain and recoiled upon the flat,
For Casey, mighty Casey, was advancing to the bat.

There was ease in Casey's manner as he stepped into his place;
There was pride in Casey's bearing and a smile on Casey's face.
And when, responding to the cheers, he lightly doffed his hat,
No stranger in the crowd could doubt 'twas Casey at the bat.

Ten thousand eyes were on him as he rubbed his hands with dirt;
Five thousand tongues applauded when he wiped them on his shirt.
Then while the writhing pitcher ground the ball into his hip,
Defiance gleamed in Casey's eye, a sneer curled Casey's lip.

And now the leather-covered sphere came hurtling through the air,
And Casey stood a-watching it in haughty grandeur there.
Close by the sturdy batsman the ball unheeded sped—
"That ain't my style," said Casey. "Strike one," the umpire said.

From the benches, black with people, there went up a muffled roar,
Like the beating of the storm-waves on a stern and distant shore.
"Kill him! Kill the umpire!" shouted someone on the stand;
And its likely they'd a-killed him had not Casey raised his hand.

With a smile of Christian charity great Casey's visage shown;
He stilled the rising tumult; he bade the game go on;
He signaled to the pitcher, and again the spheroid flew;
But Casey still ignored it, and the umpire said, "Strike two."

"Fraud!" cried the maddened thousands, and echo answered fraud;
But one scornful look from Casey and the audience was awed.
They saw his face grow stern and cold, they saw his muscles strain,
And they knew that Casey wouldn't let that ball go by again.

The sneer is gone from Casey's lip, his teeth are clenched in hate;
He pounds with cruel violence his bat upon the plate.
And now the pitcher holds the ball, and now he lets it go,
And now the air is shattered by the force of Casey's blow.

Oh, somewhere in this favored land the sun is shining bright;
The band is playing somewhere, and somewhere hearts are light,
And somewhere men are laughing, and somewhere children shout;
But there is no joy in Mudville—mighty Casey has struck out.

Ernest Lawrence Thayer

&

THE TOUCH OF THE MASTER'S HAND

*Those who aspire to biblical manhood need to be reminded that
God can take even the most rejected or wasted life and transform
it into something beautiful. No person is insignificant, if God
breathes life into him. The Lord is not only the master, but the
potter, that shapes each vessel according to his wisdom and
infinite counsel.*

Twas battered and scarred, and the auctioneer
Thought it scarcely worth his while
To waste much time on the old violin,
But he held it up with a smile.

"What am I bidden, good folks?" he cried.
"Who will start bidding for me?"
"A dollar, a dollar"—then, "Two!" "Only two?
Two dollars, and who'll make it three?
Three dollars once, three dollars, twice;
Going for three—" But no,
From the room, far back, a gray-haired man
Came forward and picked up the bow;
Then wiping the dust from the old violin
And tightening the loosened strings,

He played a melody pure and sweet,
As sweet as a caroling angel sings.

The music ceased and the auctioneer,
With a voice that was quiet and low,
Said, "What am I bidden for the old violin?"
And he held it up with the bow.
"A thousand dollars, and who'll make it two?
Two thousand! And who'll make it three?
Three thousand, once; three thousand, twice;
And going, and gone!" said he.
The people cheered, but some of them cried,
"We do not quite understand
What changed its worth?" Swift came the reply;
"The touch of the Master's hand."

And many a man with life out of tune,
And battered and scarred with sin,
Is auctioned cheap to the thoughtless crowd,
Much like the old violin.
A "mess of pottage," a glass of wine,
A game—and he travels on.
He's "going" once, and "going" twice,
He's "going" and almost "gone."
But the Master comes, and the foolish crowd
Never can quite understand
The worth of a soul, and the change that's wrought
By the touch of the Master's hand.

Myra Brooks Welch

෨

THE GODS OF THE COPYBOOK HEADINGS

*During the 19th century, students were required to learn and
memorize important truths by writing them down as axioms in
copy books. In "The Gods of the Copy Book Headings," Kipling
reveals the intellectual and moral bankruptcy of those who view
progress as a constant evolutionary process of finding new, trendy
philosophies by which to live. In the final analysis, the historic
truths of Christianity will vanquish the platitudes of modernity.*

As I pass through my incarnations in every age and race,
I make my proper prostrations to the Gods of the Market-Place.
Peering through reverent fingers I watch them flourish and fall,
And the Gods of the Copybook Headings, I notice, outlast them all.

We were living in trees when they met us. They showed us each in turn
That Water would certainly wet us, as Fire would certainly burn:
But we found them lacking in Uplift, Vision and Breadth of Mind,
So we left them to teach the Gorillas while we followed the March
    of Mankind.

We moved as the Spirit listed. They never altered their pace,
Being neither cloud nor wind-borne like the Gods of the
    Market-Place;
But they always caught up with our progress, and presently word
    would come
That a tribe had been wiped off its icefield, or the lights had gone out
    in Rome.

With the Hopes that our World is built on they were utterly out of touch.
They denied that the Moon was Stilton; they denied she was even Dutch.
They denied that Wishes were Horses; they denied that a Pig had Wings.
So we worshipped the Gods of the Market Who promised these
    beautiful things.

When the Cambrian measures were forming, They promised
    perpetual peace.
They swore, if we gave them our weapons, that the wars of the tribes
    would cease.
But when we disarmed They sold us and delivered us bound to our foe,
And the Gods of the Copybook Headings said: "Stick to the Devil
    you know."

On the first Feminian Sandstones we were promised the Fuller Life
(Which started by loving our neighbour and ended by loving his wife)
Till our women had no more children and the men lost reason and faith,
And the Gods of the Copybook Heading said: "The Wages of Sin
    is Death."

In the Carboniferous Epoch we were promised abundance for all,
By robbing selected Peter to pay for collective Paul;
But, though we had plenty of money, there was nothing our money
    could buy,
And the Gods of the Copybook Heading said: "If you don't work you die."

Then the Gods of the Market tumbled, and their smooth-tongued
    wizards withdrew,
And the hearts of the meanest were humbled and began to believe it
    was true
That All is not Gold that Glitters, and Two and Two make Four—
And the Gods of the Copybook Headings limped up to explain it
    once more.

As it will be in the future, it was at the birth of Man—
There are only four things certain since Social Progress began:—
That the Dog returns to his Vomit and the Sow returns to her Mire,
And the burnt Fool's bandaged finger goes wobbling back to the Fire;

And that after this is accomplished, and the brave new world begins
When all men are paid for existing and no man must pay for his sins,
As surely as Water will wet us, as surely as Fire will burn,
The Gods of the Copybook Headings with terror and slaughter return!

Rudyard Kipling